About the Author

Suresh Kumar is a British Indian businessman, an engaging entrepreneur, and a passionate philanthropist, born in 1963 in Ilford, Essex.

He established 'Indra Travel' in East London in 1981, a successful travel agency named in the loving memory of his mother 'Indra.' Over the years he has launched The Kumar Foundation and RCA Community Awards to raise funds for various charities. Suresh has had a keen interest in serving the local community, through his political career. Due to his charitable endeavours, Suresh has been the recipient of various accolades and awards..

From an early age, he has had an enduring love for music and the arts. Elvis Presley and Kishore Kumar are his favourite singers and has been ardent follower of Bollywood and Hollywood movies.

Follow that Dream is full of insight, revelation, self-examination, and wisdom. It charts my journey through success and challenges and the lessons learnt. I'm privileged to say, 'I have lived a life that's full.'

It is my hope that this book pushes people to 'Follow that Dream', for unless a man inspires himself to greater achievements, how can he inspire the world around him.

His greatest roles in life as a loving husband to Mona, and as a Father to two loving daughters, Megha and Ektaa.

He is always willing to assist others and values above all, his family and friendships My message to all is 'Enjoy the Gift of Life to its full!'

Acknowledgement

Mona, Megha & Ektaa Kumar

The Loves of my Life

Writing this book has taken me down memory lane and rekindled those moments in my life that were challenging and at the same time rewarding for me. Some out there may be nervous about what I might say, but I have been candid enough and truthful to relate incidents based on my recollections and knowledge. I have in no way attempted to embarrass anyone.

With time, one does not recall all events and moments as they are precisely, but I have gathered information from my files and diaries, which I have kept over the years, as markers in my life.

Thank you to Mona, Megha and Ektaa, who have kept my ship on the right course over the years. Their endless love and encouragement have always been a vital ingredient in my life.

Thank you to my publisher, Chris Day of Filament Publishing and Aditi Shah for her patience and sterling work.

Thank you to Satish Parmar, my friend for the support of my book.

My gratitude to the talented Vinai Kongara for his photography.

Dedication

This book is dedicated to my

Beloved Parents

Pandit Kul Bhushen Jasuja Bhardwaj

&

Mrs Indra Bimla Bhardwaj

May they always shine bright in the sky and watch over us.

FOLLOW THAT DREAM

Opportunity is never far from those who seek it

by Suresh Kumar

Published by
Filament Publishing Ltd
14, Croydon Road, Beddington,
Croydon, Surrey, CR0 4PA, UK

+44(0)20 8688 2598
www.filamentpublishing.com

Follow that Dream © 2023 Suresh Kumar

ISBN 978-1-915465-21-4

The right of Suresh Kumar to be identified as the author of this work has been asserted by him in accordance with the Designs and Patents Act of 1988 Section 77

Printed and bound in Great Britain by TJ Books Limited, Padstow, Cornwall

CONTENTS

Preface

"I've lived a life that's full, I've travelled each and every highway, but more, more than this, I did it my way."

As I sit here on a warm spring day, with a cool Cobra beer in hand and my family around me, I get an overwhelming feeling of gratitude, for all of life's journey. There might have been some upswings and some falls that have been tough to relive, but boy I am lucky to be able to say, "I did it my way."

Nostalgia has and always will be a very powerful emotion for me - I seek to bring back the simple, happy moments of my youth even today whether it's in my food choices, or music taste still pretty much an exclusive combination of Kishore Kumar and Elvis Presley. Perhaps I seek to relive those days of the past because it reminds me of a time when pleasure in life was derived from simple things. These moments were as simple as spending weekends with our huge family around a small house, being loud and making merry even if at times there wasn't anywhere to sit! Perhaps it's because my parents were alive then and I lost them at a relatively young age, so these nostalgic moments I relive today make me feel close to them and keep their memory alive. Whatever the reason, I am at my happiest when I have my family around me, and we are discussing tales of old. I feel it's important that we stay connected to these times since they made us who we are today.

Putting this book together has been no mean feat - it has been a labour of love spanning well over a decade of handwritten musings on scraps of paper to the finished version which you are holding in your hands today. The journey hasn't always been plain sailing, but I am happy that these stories will now be shared.

It is my hope that this honest account of struggle, achievement and survival may strike a chord with some of you. I strongly feel it is by appreciating the past and where one has come from that really allows us to make the most of the present and enables us to direct where we want to go in the future. This journey has allowed me to delve into the yesteryears, reflect with family and friends on old stories and capture them for evermore in this book before they get lost in the passage of time. It has been a reflective process on mistakes made, achievements won, and lessons learnt. Through writing this book, it has allowed me to take stock of where I am today and where I see myself in life's coming chapters.

Friends, I hope you enjoy the ride and pick some useful content from this book.

Chapter 1

The Partition & New Beginnings

"There would be no cloud-nine days without rock-bottom moments left below."

-Richelle E. Goodrich

*T*he *Land of Five Rivers,* as it is called, Punjab is a beautiful and mesmerising state in the North-Western part of India, located 380 kms and a 7-hour drive from the capital, New Delhi. Considered as having the best infrastructure in India, this lush bountiful land ranks amongst the most primaeval civilisations globally, having the oldest and richest cultures in the world. Not only this, but the state is rich in religious diversity since it's the origin of various religious movements. If you ever get a chance to visit this land, you would be surprised by its diversity and exceptionality that is reflected in everything from Punjabi poetry, philosophy, devoutness, education, creativity, music, cuisine, science, technology, martial combat, structural design, ethnicities, beliefs to the long-stretched history.

The British gave up India because World War II had severely damaged the British Empire in terms of economy. To cut their losses they were forced to relinquish many of their colonies.

The British Raj was the rule of the British Crown on the Indian subcontinent; it is also called Crown rule in India, or Direct rule in India, and lasted for 89 years from 1858 to 1947.

Clement Attlee, the Prime Minister of the United Kingdom, announced on 20th February 1947 that: The British Government would grant full self-government to India by 30th June 1948 at the latest.

On June 3rd 1947, in a joint conference with the Congress Party and the Muslim League, the last Viceroy of India, Louis Mountbatten, announced the partition of India. This was known as the "Mountbatten Plan". Both the Congress leaders and the Muslim League accepted it. According to the Mountbatten Plan, the country would be divided into Hindu India and Muslim East Pakistan, now Bangladesh, and Pakistan. Crudely, this was a division based upon religious affiliation, the only time in history, with the creation of a Muslim majority in West and East Pakistan and a Hindu majority in India. Over two million lives were lost.

Pakistan became an independent country on 14th August whereas India celebrated independence on 15th August 1947. India won its independence from the British. This was a very important moment in history. The British finally left.

But partition triggered riots, mass casualties, and a colossal wave of migration. Millions of people moved to what they hoped would be safer territory, with Muslims heading towards Pakistan, and Hindus and Sikhs in the direction of India. It was the largest, most abrupt, unplanned, and tragic transfer of population ever seen.

Thousands of people who managed to cross the border lived their life as refugees and in refugee camps. Thousands of women were abducted and there was no trace of them.

As I cover this most traumatic episode in the history of India. I write each word with tears in my eyes, sadness fills my heart. Although, I was not present in 1947, not even born, the magnitude of the passage of history, shakes me to the core.

India and Pakistan are neighbours, born to one Mother, India. I pray one day they will live like brothers and sisters, in love and tranquillity. Only time has divided us. We are one, we speak a similar language, we look similar, and we eat the same food, and so on. Maybe I will not see this in my lifetime but pray and hope that in the future our two nations become one. If that were to happen, with belief and determination, no country can stand in our way of progression and success. But this will only come from the will of the people, it is they who hold destiny in their hands.

At the core of this beautiful land lies a story of a family caught amidst the heart-breaking tragedies of the 1947 partition. Friends became foes, and families became strangers - events that would set in motion a changed course of history and would forever divide once-beloved communities.

My mother's family was from Lyallpur, now Faisalabad in Pakistan. They were one of the millions of such families, who were forced to leave everything behind overnight, and travel to India.

My grandfather and father were working in Lahore at the time of partition, even though the family roots were originally based in Kitna, Punjab, India. They also returned to Kitna just before partition.

When our forefathers put down roots in rural places, the thing that allowed them to survive was that they had faith to see them through the tough times. The belief in themselves would carry generations through obstacles, a commodity which would be relied upon through many trials and tribulations in the future.

My great grandfather, Pandit Ditta Ram, was an official Astrologer for The Maharajah of Punjab, Ranjit Singh and gave several years of service. As a gift for his loyal service and tenure, he was gifted 625 acres of land in Punjab. Over time some of the land was sold and the proceeds were invested in various projects. One such project was a Mill in Mumbai, and later the investment multiplied and he cashed in. It is said that he brought silver and gold coins on horseback to the village of Kitna.

Our great grandfather supported many villagers with his wealth, and he would loan monies and the locals would deposit their land deeds with him as collateral. But he never transferred the deeds over to his name, but instead kept them safely, to be returned to the owners. He was not a loan shark but just wished to assist his local community.

Sadly, he was not too secure with money and due to disputes and false claims by certain people, he spent close to 20 years fighting litigation in the courts. This exhausted much of the accumulated wealth and most of the investments were lost due to the passage of time.

My father was the son of Smt Banti Devi, a homemaker and Pandit Kali Sharan, a proud railway driver. He was born in Lahore, Pakistan. Sadly in 1952 our grandmother Banti Devi Bhardwaj suddenly passed away after being bitten by a snake and developing a serious infection.

In 1940, my grandfather Pandit Kali Sharan travelled to Lahore looking for better job opportunities and spent some time there and gradually called my father and the family to join him in 1940, where he spent a short time working at Jasuja Shoe Company. It was difficult to get a job, even though he was well educated and spoke good English. In 1941, some friends suggested that he meet Gautam Jasuja, Manager of Bata Shoe Company in Lahore, a caring man, who after meeting our father, wished to help him and was fond of him. They developed a brotherly love for each other. So, they both made a plan, that my father would change his name to Kul Bhushan Jasuja and drop the Bhardwaj surname for this mission. Gautam, advised Bata Shoe, that Kul Bhushan was his younger brother, hence it was easier to secure employment.

My father secured employment with Bata Shoe Company in Lahore and began work as an assistant and learnt the craft and techniques of selling. Even in later years, when my father had travelled to London and began a new life, he maintained the name Jasuja, as a mark of respect to his dear friend Gautam.

As partition gradually came closer and was becoming a reality and its actual effects on India were being felt, there was much unrest, across the country, especially in Lahore and families started to take sides and head for their destination. In early August 1947, my father sent his wife and a young two-month-old Raj, back to Kitna, Punjab, India. They were to travel from Lahore to Amritsar by train and by bus from Amritsar to Jalandhar and then finally onward to Kitna. Due to tension and unrest on the route, my mother could not get the train, as they were jam-packed and instead took the train to Lyallpur, Faisalabad. She had travelled to her parent's house and joined them for passage to Punjab, as the family was well-connected locally. They took a train from Lyallpur to Amritsar and along the way, there were some disturbances and rioters fired gunshots at the train. Many travellers took cover, but my mother took up a rifle, that had fallen to the floor after an army soldier had been hit. She fired back at the rebel looters and rioters. My mother had fired guns, as taught by Kali Sharan, our grandfather, sometime earlier in Kitna.

On 14th August 1947, two days prior to partition, my father and Uncle Varinder, his younger brother tried in desperation to flee Lahore for Amritsar, due to the fighting, unrest and killings. On route to the Lahore train station, they were stopped and questioned, as barricades were set up to stop Hindus from fleeing Pakistan. They were asked Hindu or Muslim? My father hesitated and quickly replied Muslim and showed them a tattoo he had made on his left inside arm that had the initials A.B, meaning Ali Baksh. In fact, the initials should have been tattooed K.B. for Kul Bhushen, my father's first name, but the tattoo artist made a mistake and dad never got around to changing the initials. That saved the day, and they were allowed to continue their journey. I recall that dad had said that there were so many dead bodies scattered on the journey to the Lahore train station, lying on the floor of the station and the tracks. People were being slaughtered and this was total madness on both sides. My father never changed the initials tattooed on his arm and kept them as a memory of the challenging times he had faced.

My father, Pandit Kul Bhushen, and mother, Indra Bimla Bhardwaj, were survivors of the 1947 partition. A time when houses were burnt to the ground, bloodshed was rife, and families were desperately searching for safe passage - my grandparents and parents were amongst many on the platforms of the railway lines waiting to escape the bloodshed and escape Lahore to Punjab. My father was a humble and hardworking man. Before the partition, my dad had a steady job as a manager for Bata Shoe Company in Lahore. He was educated and he regularly assisted others, with writing letters and dealing with day-to-day formalities, in which he took much pride. He was honest, honourable and was held in high esteem in the community.

Whilst writing this story, my memory turned the pages to a popular Kishore Kumar song from the Hindi film Hum Sab Ustad Hain, "Pyar Bantte Chalo, translates to Spread Love" This is my message to all.

Our family roots were well established in Kitna, Punjab upon arriving in Kitna once again, establishing themselves in a small village, my father, with his excellent record at Bata Shoe in Lahore, continued working as a Manager of Bata Shoe Company, now in Jalandhar Cantt, until a close relation betrayed him. With a selfish entrepreneurial vision, that relation devised a scheme to make a quick buck by removing shoes from their boxes and selling them independently to recoup losses made in his business, leaving empty boxes behind in the store. Shortly afterwards, when an audit was conducted, this incident came to light, and my father took the blame. The audit exposed a shortfall of 4500 Indian Rupees, a significant amount in those days, which today amounts to approximately £50, not to forget these were also challenging times. It would be a possible Police case and humiliation. To avoid prosecution, my father was given ten days to clear his debt owed to Bata Shoe Company and to resign gracefully. As the payment deadline approached, my father could not raise the shortfall and never revealed who had done this - his trait of generosity shining through.

He knew that there is no foundation like honesty and fairness - two principles that he had built his life on alongside his faith in God. As a result, two friends of my father, jewellers from Jalandhar named Kura Mal, and Inder, knowing that my dad, was innocent, offered to pay the debt on behalf of my father, avoiding any further humiliation. Due to the circumstances, my father had to hand in his resignation, which led to more hardship at home. Subsequently, the two friends were reimbursed by my father, with sincere gratitude and a lifelong friendship.

Struggling to take care of our growing family, my father took any and every job to make ends meet and support his wife and children. He began working as a car cleaner and waited on cars for wealthy individuals attending theatres and parties. Heavily reliant on tips, some people used to give him money in small change, and some would go by without providing any tip. One of the heart-breaking memories I recall was a story he told us. One time, he cleaned a car outside a casino and waited for the owner to return. After ten hours, the owner finally appeared and had a bad night gambling and was in no mood to offer any tips or acknowledge my dad's hard work. He drove off and disregarded my father's humble requests for a tip. My dad was shattered that day as tips equalled food on the table. It was moments like this that fuelled my father's desire to challenge his life's destiny and change the course of his life and search for new horizons.

Money had never been a free commodity in our household, and the family faced many hardships. We were a large family, and being the eldest sibling, my father was the provider to many, including the wedding expenses of his four sisters and three brothers. This might sound a little strange to you, but family bonds are very powerful in the subcontinent. In the fifties, women were considered homemakers, and men, the financial providers of the family. Times were difficult, but they did not always stay the same. My dad marched onto better days soon.

My mother's family consisted of her father Jamna Das Sanger and mother Lakshmi Devi and had four sons and four daughters. The oldest brother, Roop Lal Sanger, who lived in Apra, Punjab, had an immigration and passport business. He provided passports and travel documents to people looking for opportunities abroad. At that juncture, people in India were looking for new beginnings in a hunt to venture out to foreign countries for an enhanced standard of life, a regular talking point between siblings in the Bhardwaj household.

In 1954, my parents resided in Kitna, Punjab, and at that time had three children, Raj, Surinder, more commonly known as Tony, and Satish, respectively 7, 4, and 2 years old. My elder brother, Raj had been schooling in Kitna, Apra and Garshankar, in Punjab and was sent to Apra, one summer to stay with my mother's family in the hopes that he would become more worldly-wise. Soon after reaching there, he became close to our uncles, Roop Lal, Joginder Sanger, and our cousin, Kewal Sanger, son of Roop Lal.

In the 1950s, many left their homes in India, looking for better prospects worldwide. Some ventured out to America, Canada, Europe, and the most popular place was Great Britain, by aeroplane. In those early days of aviation, it would take around fifteen hours, for the flight duration.

In March 1954, my father applied for clearance to the Prime Minister's office, Government of India for a visa to the United States of America. The application was rejected, and he was dismayed. Life would have worked out differently if we had settled in the US.

My father took many trips between Apra and Kitna this summer on his bicycle in the scorching heat of an Indian summer. He spent hours conversing with Uncle Roop Lal over the sounds of a bubbling hookah pipe and the slurps of Masala Chai, which ultimately led to the decision that my father would fly to Great Britain and look at the potential of a better life in a new settlement. The idea was simple; he would go alone at the outset, and the family would follow if all worked out well. Uncle Roop Lal was asked to take care of all the official procedures and arrange my father's travel passage. My parents had very little money to pay for the travel, so they borrowed money from him, which was later recompensed fully. He was generous, compassionate, worldly wise and full of hope for his family.

With dreams of a better life sparkling in my dad's eyes, my father embarked on a gruelling trip from Kitna to Phagwara by road, then by train to Delhi, and finally to Bombay to take his first-ever flight. I often think about what his thought process would have been, entering an airport for the first time to board TWA flight 905 on 25th February 1955 from Santa Cruz Airport – Mumbai to London, departing at 22:00 and leaving behind all that he ever knew. He had never travelled on an aircraft nor left India.

To ensure a smooth transition into his new life, Uncle Roop Lal had acquaintances in London to whom he had introduced my father, along with other individuals who had left Punjab in search of a better life in the United Kingdom. He decided to stay with known associates at 38 Princelet Street in Aldgate, East London. His new humble abode was built over the ground, first and second floors and 16 people were sharing its facilities. It was not a luxurious place to live but merely a place to stay warm and sleep for the night after a hard day's work. His first observation was that London was smoggy and much polluted. The air was not clean. New horizons in London were no bed of roses or paved with Gold.

Finding a job as a door-to-door salesman, and obtaining a Pedlars Certificate my father and his friends worked alternate shifts – morning, evening, and night so that the beds could be shared in rotation one shift after another. London winter nights were fierce in those days, maybe even more than now, since a lot has changed due to global warming. Cold and rainy weather used to take charge of the city, where freezing temperatures were not uncommon, and snow was not unheard of. At times, the only way to keep warm was to have a weekly pint of Guinness at the local pub- a hobby my father enjoyed with his friends. My father worked long hours - day in and day out, fully aware that he had a family back home in Kitna to support and who was waiting for his weekly money order to survive.

In 1959, my father was employed with J G Ingram and Son Ltd, for a short while as my father returned to Punjab to arrange the wedding of his younger brother, Varinder, to Prakash, the younger sister of my mother, Indra Sharma Bhardwaj. Hence, two brothers got married to two sisters. In 1960, my father and Uncle Varinder returned to the U.K. to continue their hunt for enhanced opportunities. After some time, things had started to turn out for the better, and plans were on the move to send my mum and now, the four kids as Ashok had arrived in May 1960, to live with my dad in the U.K.

In 1961, My dad's younger brother Varinder's wife Prakash and her one-year-old daughter Riya travelled to London and stayed at Broomhill Road, Goodmayes. They purchased 102 Pembroke Road, Seven Kings, in 1964, where all the family moved. My Auntie Prakash was a skilled machinist, who worked for top brands and the latest fashion designers. She was close to my mother and spent a lot of time together. In later years when my mother detected lumps under her arms, she first confided in Auntie Prakash, which was later diagnosed as breast cancer.

My mother along with her four young children was still in Kitna. A young woman alone in a small village in Punjab was a sensitive cause during those years. My mother had to fend for her four children and an ageing father-in-law, along with taking care of day-to-day tasks in a village predominantly ruled by men. My mum was a fierce and determined woman who, with the backing of my grandfather, was both loved and respected in the village. My Uncle and Aunties, the first generation, were determined, loving, progressive, caring, courageous, hardworking, inspirational, and devoted to their children. They made many sacrifices for the young ones and even went without the luxury to ensure their children had enough, and we never felt that anything was missing from our lives.

In 1961, my father commenced work at The Ford Motor Company in Dagenham, Essex, where he would remain till 1973. He enjoyed working and made some new friends. But at times, the work was hard, as he worked in the engine plant. He worked long shifts and always put in for overtime to make that little extra money.

Documentation and plans were in progress for my mum with her four kids to join my father in London. Passports had to be obtained. Uncle Roop Lal proved to be incredibly supportive during this time. Passport requirements had been completed and were to be collected from Hoshiarpur, a nearby town. When our mother got there, she was advised that the passports were ready for collection in Jalandhar City, Punjab, 60 kilometres away. Never one to be reliant, my mother set off alone on foot to the bus stand and took a bus to Jalandhar City. My siblings were left with my grandfather. As the day progressed, there was no news of our mother. As night fell, darkness began to creep in, panic was rife in the Bhardwaj house as there was no word of my mother's whereabouts. Raj, now 14, was tough, sturdy, and strong built. He set off late into the evening from the village with one of his friends on his bicycle, looking for our mother. Frantically searching through the fields, Raj bellowed my mother's name to no avail.

Tired and desperate to reach home, my mother heard advancing footsteps towards her and took shelter in the foothills of a wheat field. Fast approaching midnight in the light of the moon, she heard a familiar voice echoing her name. The feared footsteps were those of my brother Raj.

From this day on, Raj became her protector. Strong as she was, my mother always knew she could rely on Raj to support her. With passports in hand, my family was ready to make their first flight to London, packing all their worldly possessions into one suitcase between them.

Tied to the history of his land, my grandfather, Kali Sharan, decided to stay back in Kitna, Punjab. As they say, the soil is very rich in the subcontinent. Our grandfather Kali Sharan was attached to Raj, my elder brother, and when saying his final farewell to our mother and her young children, he said to Raj, I am not going to see you again, so look after everyone. He was 82 years old.

Auntie Swarna Devi, the wife of my father's younger brother Uncle Naresh, moved to Kitna, from Gharshankar with their family to support and look after our grandfather. Upon reflection, he should not have stayed behind and voyaged to London with the rest of his family. However, the prospects of a new life were not so appealing to a man who had fought through the partition years and witnessed the turn of the century and its event.

First time on an aeroplane, on 27th May 1962, my mother, dressed in a sari, along with her four sons, Raj, Surinder aka Tony, Satish and Ashok left India and arrived in London via Paris on Air France on 28th May 1962. My brother, Satish, a mere ten years old at the time-joyfully recalled the air flight attendants wearing black netted stockings, going all the way up their legs. Mum and the four young boys never ate on the plane, as they thought it would cost them extra money for the food being served. They should have advised them that the food was included in the ticket price.

When they arrived, my father had already secured a permanent job at Ford Motor Company. He had a job in the engine plant and worked a very long shift, and he took regular overtime at every opportunity to earn extra money. Our roots were now established in East London.

In 1964 Naresh Chander Bhardwaj, my dad's younger brother, travelled to London to join the growing Bhardwaj clan, for better prospects. My dad had made all the arrangements for his passage, and he too stayed in the joint family home at Broomhill Road, Goodmayes and in 1968 Auntie Swarna and the children, Sumna, Roman, Rakesh, Harish and Mohan, also boarded a flight from India for London, to support her husband Naresh and commence new beginnings.

Once again, the family was united. As my father had started to experience a level of success from his time in London, he was determined to support the rest of his extended family in making a move to the UK. He encouraged more and more of his relatives to take the opportunity to settle in Great Britain. He made way for his brothers, Varinder Kumar and Naresh Chander, and their families to arrive in the U.K. and settle there.

Our father, also called his sister's family, Bimla and Bhagwant Kalia, starting with the eldest son Om Parkash Kalia who was born in 1940 in Gharshankar, Punjab, in March 1962. Followed by Tarsem Kalia in September 1962 and their families. They also ventured to London, for better prospects. Initially, some stayed at Broomhill Road, Goodmayes and then as the family grew more prominent, they moved in 1964 to 27 Airthrie Road, Goodmayes, which was purchased for £4600 and another property at number 50, for £3600 which was renovated, as by now all the family had migrated to Great Britain.

In 1971, the Kalia family set up a grocery shop Sam Food Stores on Goodmayes Road, Goodmayes, then established Sam Travel and Tarsem Kalia and Santosh Kalia, his wife set up Kalljet Travel in Manor Park.

In later years, my cousin O.P Kalia was instrumental in establishing The Radha Krishna Hindu Mandir, on Cedars Road, Stratford, in the London Borough of Newham. Along with Mr Goyal, Mohan Sharma and my brother Raj Kumar and other supporters. Donations were sought from family and friends and soon a loan of £15,000 was repaid to Midland Bank. Initially, the Mandir opened on Sundays for two hours and religious musical programmes were commenced on a regular basis. Food was served to the devotees, to encourage people to attend.

My cousin Om Parkash, a wise and worldly man regularly quotes "Don't listen to anyone; listen to your heart and do well and support all."

My elder brother Raj was hardworking and had an eye for the good things life offered. In 1962, Raj and Surinder started schooling at Mayfield High School in Goodmayes, and Satish attended Goodmayes Primary School. After one year, Satish was to follow them to Mayfield High School. Raj left Mayfield after a month or so. Our father's income needed to be supported and Raj decided to drop schooling and get employment. He worked various jobs, in 1962, General Engineering in Hainault, in 1963, Nucky Scott at Enfield, in 1964, Wonder Loaf – Bread factory in Becontree Heath, 1964, Lacrinoid Plastic Factory in Gidea Park. Raj was dedicated and knew too well that he had to support his parents and young brothers. He would put in for overtime, at every given opportunity, to make extra money. Our mother and father really appreciated all that Raj was doing and making many sacrifices for his family.

With a focus on supporting the family income, Raj took very little schooling and instead enrolled in evening classes. Furthermore, he worked in various occupations to earn additional funds for the family and to support my dad.

With the '60s being live and let live, it's surprising how racism and bullying were in full colour throughout society and schools. Subject to taunts and jibes by their peers, my brothers and their friends put a few noses out of place and soon taught these bullies a good lesson. There was no messing with the Punjabi boys from India.

With most of our families having relocated to the UK from Punjab, initially, they lived jointly in rented accommodation at 12 Broomfield Road, Goodmayes, and a large triple-fronted house. As the families were rapidly growing, space became tight, which led to tensions in the household. During this time, after a rare drinking session, my dad's two brothers, Naresh and Varinder started a fight with dad. Raj, who was now old enough, had to intervene and, with the aid of a broomstick, broke up the argument. From that time onwards, everyone became aware that it was not a good idea to pick on my dad. He was not the aggressive type and avoided confrontation. He was soft and gentle.

With living space now, a rare commodity, it became apparent that more space was needed, and it was time to move out and get a place. Mum and dad bought our first freehold house in the U.K., at 9 Highbury Gardens, Ilford, Essex, for the grand sum of £2200 in August 1963, the year I was born. Although the families had separated, the relationships were strong. It was a weekly trend to gather around at our house on Fridays and spend the entire weekend together. All the men folk gathered and went to a local pub, The Cauliflower on High Road, Ilford. There was much love and affection between the families. They supported each other, if one were in need, they would all muster together and help. This was a joint family system in fruition.

I fondly remember those evenings spent in the car park of the pub where all the youngsters in the family ran around playing catch and chase where we were intermittently treated to bags of walkers' crisps and a bottle of light ale beer to share amongst us all. I recall peeking into the pub, living on the edge, and seeing rounds of 20 pints at a time being ordered. This was our weekly highlight.

When the closing bell rang at The Cauliflower, we would saunter back home for an evening slap-up meal waiting for us, courtesy of the ladies of the household. Plenty of meat and vegetable dishes to go around- the smiles of our mothers always disguised the hard work that went into supporting the family. Everyone used to leave in the early hours, well-fed and, looking forward to meeting the next weekend. I recall a famous hit song from the 1960s, 'Those were the days my friend' sung by Mary Hopkins.

Like the Jewish community, the Indians were no different and established themselves in a similar way. Whatever trade and commerce one would begin, the others sought to trail. Accordingly, if we bought a grocery shop, others would want to start the same. If a Travel Agency was established by one of the family members, others started one as well. All the family members did well and started to earn good money. Life was now starting to fall into place for all the families that had arrived in the U.K.

In the late 1960s, our parents faced further challenges and the United Kingdom faced a serious dilemma.

Enoch Powell, Rivers of Blood, his speech strongly criticised mass immigration, to the United Kingdom and the proposed Race Relations Bill. Powell, a prominent member of the Tories for more than 20 years – took a stand against the growing numbers of non-native citizens in Britain.

He voiced concerns over immigration: "They found their wives unable to obtain hospital beds in childbirth and at work they found that employers hesitated to apply to the immigrant worker the standards of discipline and competence required." One of the more controversial suggestions was that continuous immigration would lead to violence as well as prejudice towards 'native' British citizens. He called for voluntary repatriation for those who would be happy to return to the countries of their birth. In 1968, Powell's inflammatory rhetoric comments, got him axed from the Tory Cabinet. In the aftermath of Powell's inflammatory speech, which split the nation and instantly became one of modern British history's most divisive addresses, the fallout was swift and fierce. Protesters took to the streets in support of Powell's backing for the repatriation of immigrants. Powell was cast out of the Conservative shadow cabinet, effectively ending his political ambitions. Almost overnight, it was placed on the frontline of a national debate about immigration, integration and race relations.

"Enoch Powell was wrong about Britain". Where? he predicted 'rivers of blood', people of different colours and creeds have mixed and learned to live together and in harmony. We have largely moved on from the racism of the 60s and 70s, and young Britons have higher expectations of our society, and they deserve to be met.

The strong determination of the families was unparalleled and the survival instinct intact to support each member of the family, to succeed and with an unmatched spirit of generosity.

There are stories of early settlers in London from India, who were married in India and travelled to the UK, for better prospects. They had girlfriends and remarried local girls and settled in London. They forget that they had responsibilities and commitments in India with their families. They were overwhelmed with the way of life and started new families. On the other hand, there were also the majority who fulfilled their responsibility and stayed loyal and faithful.

Many early settlers abroad, who would have left India for new beginnings, would miss their families back home and my mind turns to the famous lines from the legendary Filmi lyricist Anand Bakshi, Chitthi aayee hai wattan se chitthi aayee hai means A letter has arrived, a memory of the love has arrived.

Dad's TWA Flight Seat Number

Dad's TWA Flight Ticket Front Cover

Dad's TWA Flight Ticket

Dad's TWA Flight Ticket Boarding Pass

Dad & Mum 1980

Naresh Uncle, Dad and Varinder Uncle Dad's Brothers

Chapter 2

The Early Years

On 15th February 1963, I was born at the Ilford Maternity Hospital, Eastern Avenue Ilford. I was the first in the family to be born in the U.K. and was told that it was very cold with the worst snow showers ever recorded.

1963 was indeed a year of events. Elvis Presley was in Hollywood, making movies; the Beatles were conquering the world, with their new brand of music; Cliff Richard was on a Summer Holiday; Muhammad Ali, aka Cassius Clay, was soon to become the heavyweight champ of the world; Rajesh Khanna was just finding his way into some part-time theatre work in Mumbai, soon to become Superstar of Indian Cinema in Bollywood and not to forget the assassination of JFK - John Fitzgerald Kennedy and the famous speech of Dr Martin Luther King I have a Dream. Roger Moore aka Simon Templar had begun a popular TV Series called The Saint on ITV. Sean Connery - James Bond 007 was to release the second Bond film - From Russia with Love. My favourite bond has to be - Roger Moore because of his charm and easy-going wit. A son of a Policeman from South London. He was tall and handsome, a perfect gentleman, and he gave the Bond films a touch of class, starting with Live and Let Die in 1972. We used to look out for the Bond movies, full of adventure and fun packed. The Aston Martin DB5 had many gadgets, including tire-slashing hubcaps, twin front-mounted machine guns, an ejector seat, bulletproof shields, a car phone (unheard of at the time!), bumper rams, and a mechanism that could dispense oil slick or smoke and other gadgets were a treat to watch.

Not surprisingly, I don't have much recollection of my early years before the age of 6 in 1969.

My 6th birthday in 1969 was an eventful one for me, mainly because I received an Elvis LP, titled Let's Be Friends from my brother, Ashok. He gave it to me as a gift, but I suspect it was more of a gift for himself, as he later took it back from me. Nevertheless, it was a prized possession repeatedly played on a turn-style record player, which we had at 9 Highbury Gardens. My love and enduring admiration for Elvis was born and will last forever. Elvis Presley greatly influenced me during my childhood.

We resided at 9 Highbury Gardens, it was a small three-bedroom house just off the High Road in Ilford and Green Lane in Ilford, Essex. As you would enter the house, there was a small front garden, then stepping into the house a small lobby will greet you. To the left was a living room and behind that a bedroom/prayer room, which my parents used. Krishan and I slept there. Krishan with my mother and I with my dad, in two separate double beds. Walking to the rear was a dining cum kitchen and an outside toilet, which I called a John. As you would enter the front door, to the right was a staircase leading to the first floor, and to the left a small box room, which was Satish's room. Next to his room was Raj's room and then Tony's and Ashok's room, followed by a double bathroom.

In the garden, we had a shed, which the young called The Bat Cave. There was a coal bunker and a large garden, where my parents grew vegetables. I inherited the love of gardening from my parents. I find it to be cathartic and therapeutic.

My father worked at the Ford Motor Company in Dagenham, Essex. He left early in the morning and returned home late at night since he would put in extra overtime. He could not drive and travelled from Green Lane on the 86 or 25 bus, to Dagenham in Essex. My mother would rise early to pack some lunch for my father and get ready to set the kids on their way. With all this going on, it would be an understatement if I said that our parents had a hectic routine. Moreover, we did not have much money, but by the grace of the Almighty, we always had enough to go around. In those days we could not afford a washing machine and all the clothes were washed by hand by our mother. Our parents never let us feel how tough things were for them and we never felt deprived of anything. That was the charm of my childhood. My parents were amazing, and I would pray to God, that I am born to them again in my reincarnation. Next time around I would want to make sure that they enjoy all the luxury that life has to offer. They deserved no less.

Despite taking some driving lessons from a colleague at work, my father was never confident behind the wheel of a car. He used public transport and was happy, nonetheless.

In 1965, two years after I was born, whilst working at Ford, my father purchased a new car for Raj. He got an employee discount. It was a brand-new blue colour, Ford Anglia bought for a total of £528.00 straight from the showroom. Reg. No MEV 737 C, the car was Raj's pride and delight.

In 1965 my younger brother Krishan was born on 28th December at the Ilford Maternity Hospital, Eastern Avenue, Ilford.

A favourite TV series Thunderbirds debuted in September 1965 on the ITV network. The series was exported to around 30 countries during the 1960s. Periodically repeated, it was adapted for radio in the 1990s and has influenced many TV programmes and other media. Set in the year 2060, Thunderbirds Are Go follows the exploits of the Tracy brothers - Scott, Virgil, Alan, Gordon, and John - who form the backbone of International Rescue a life-saving organisation that operates from a hidden base in the Southern Pacific Ocean, and who save people from disasters and danger.

Krishan, my younger brother and I would act out scenes from the show. He would act as Virgil Tracey of Thunderbird 2 and me as Scott Tracey of Thunderbird 1.

In 1967, Surinder Desour, a travel agent running Continental Travel, based at 6 Brick Lane, Aldgate, left for India due to a family emergency at short notice. He asked his friend Joginder Sanger to buy him out. A deal was struck at £3500. Uncle had £2000 saved, and he borrowed £1500 from my father, as he had savings, which was subsequently returned with gratitude and thanks.

At the request of Uncle Joginder, in 1968, my brother Satish joined Eastways Travel in Brick Lane, in East London, as a part-time worker initially and then full-time. In 1970, Raj also joined the travel industry at Eastways Travel. Satish worked in the office, looking after the day-to-day business, and Raj was visiting different airline and travel offices. In particular, he was making valuable links that would be convenient and useful in the future.

1969 saw Raj marry Urmil Tiwari from Jalandhar, Punjab. Raj was a young and good-looking man who knew how to charm his way in life. The marriage was held in Jalandhar, Punjab, India. Krishan and my mother went to Jalandhar in 1968 for the preparations, and I followed with my father. We were away for around eight months or so.

I had my first flight in late 1968 with BOAC airlines. The plane had a stopover, I remember it was snowing heavily in Luxembourg. However, upon arriving in Bombay, we really felt the heat. From Bombay, we took a local Air India flight to Delhi, followed by a long journey in a taxi as we had to travel by road to Apra and then to Chandigarh. My Uncle Desraj Sanger, my mother's elder brother, lived in Chandigarh with his wife, Prema, and two sons, Rocky and Ruby. Sadly, in years to come, Rocky passed away in Delhi.

I recall that after arriving at Apra in the early hours of the morning, my father realised that he had forgotten his treasured half bottle of English whisky in the back of the taxi. So, he burst out, abusing the taxi driver, who by now was well on his way to Delhi, perhaps enjoying the imported whisky. Apra, in Punjab, was the home of my mother's family, after they left Pakistan after the partition. I still remember that when we arrived for the first time, I saw concrete steps leading to a set of metal gates that led to the veranda. It was like a courtyard of sorts.

Krishan, my younger brother was good company in India, and Satish had sent gifts for both of us through dad. A Simon Templer, Roger Moore white model Volvo from the TV series The Saint, which was very popular at the time in the 60s, for Krishan my younger brother and a model beige US Chevrolet for me. Satish was a caring brother who always looked after the younger siblings. These were great to have, and we would race the cars down the slight slopes and concrete floors in the open rooms of the courtyard in Apra.

My cousin, Rocky, who lived in Chandigarh, loved collecting bird eggs. He had a great collection of birds' eggs, all labelled in a neat wooden box, which was compartmentalised, with different birds' eggs. I had fun with Rocky and Ruby, they showed me around Chandigarh.

We shuttled between Chandigarh, where our Uncle Desraj lived with his family, and Apra in Punjab, where my grandparents lived, it was the first time I met my mother's parents. They were both very loving and caring. My mother bragged about Krishan and me in the village. She was a proud mother and protected her sons with the look of a lioness. She was a very strong woman and did not stand any nonsense.

At Raj and Urmil's wedding in January 1969, I was the best man and in Hindu customs called the Sarvala. Urmil was well educated, smart and she gave much support during the Chandigarh house-building period to my father. In August 1969 she travelled to London to be with Raj and here again she became a strong pillar of support for my mother.

In 1969, our father purchased a plot of land at House No 3122, Sector 21D, in Chandigarh, close to Piccadilly Hotel. Chandigarh in Haryana was a modern and advancing city. It was a 5-hour drive from New Delhi and a 5-hour drive to Amritsar. It was centrally located, and my father desired to return someday and live in Punjab, India. I guess "Home is where the heart is". He built a 5-bedroom luxury house, which took approximately eight months to construct. He did all the design work and purchases for the workers. He was disciplined and hard-working. I guess he always wanted to return to India in the back of his mind. India was home for him. All done simply by him moving around on a bicycle and supervising the labour and building his house in Chandigarh.

Our father rented the property to the Haryana Government in Chandigarh and got very little rent for it. When they left after several years, it was a total disaster. Our father was devastated and decided to sell it. He bore a heavy loss. Once the construction in Chandigarh was finished, we returned to London.

From 1969-1973, my mum and dad started a food and grocery business, K.B. Foods, at 343 Green Lane, Seven Kings, as suggested by Uncle Vidya Sagar, who had experience from Bradford, running a grocery store, named Himalayans Stores and it was suggested that there would be a good return, in the investment. At that time, dad was still employed at Ford Motor Company and worked shifts while my mum worked at the shop. After school, Ashok, Krishan, and I used to help in the shop with odd jobs like filling orders, looking after the counter, arranging deliveries, and other similar things. After college, Tony and my cousin Satish Sagar used to do the delivery drop-off-rounds door to door. There was a particular house on Eastern Avenue that they loved visiting for reasons best known to themselves.

During the shop period, Urmil gave much support to my mother, by looking after the house, and taking care of all the shopping, as there were many mouths to feed, including the adult members and the young children, by now Raj and Urmil had children, Kavita and Rumita were born, and then Bobby followed, along with Ashok, Krishan, and myself. It was a full house and very challenging for her at times, having recently come from Punjab-India. She handled everything in style, grace and elegance. Urmil was by now a firm pillar of the Bhardwaj Family foundation.

In 1972, the grocery shop's stocks needed to be replenished. Cash and carry were usually done on the weekends and one Sunday morning, my father, mother, Satish, Uncle Varinder who was driving and his wife Prakash. They were in a small Ford van and headed off to Nurdin Peacock cash and carry. On the return journey home to the shop in Green Lane my Uncle Varinder failed to stop at a give-way junction in Becontree Heath, and a car hit the side of the van at full speed, and the van tumbled and rolled over. They were all shaken and in shock but walked away from the horrific car crash with minor bruises and cuts. All the groceries were spewed on the road. It was a close save and a lucky escape. It could have been the beginning of the end for them.

In the early 1970s, we were young kids, and our regular keep fit routine would be to visit our local parks; South Park on Water Lane, Seven Kings Park entrance at Wallington Road or Seven Kings Little Park on Meads Lane, Valentines Park on Cranbrook Road and Hainault Forest Park in Hainault.

We were all youngsters in a similar age bracket. We were full of energy, and during the summer months, we used to get plenty of sunshine and fresh air.

On one occasion, I recall Ashok, Riya, and I were at South Park at Water Lane, and the sky was blue, the park smelled of summer scents, the grass was green, and flower beds were blooming. The lake in the centre of the park was an attraction, and kids would bring model boats and ships in the water. There was a kid showing off his remote-controlled boat and everyone wanted a closer look, so we all gathered around the edge of the lake on the concrete border. There was a sudden rush from the kids behind us, and I fell into the lake. I could not swim, and I was shouting and splashing in the water. The water was not deep, but my feet did not touch the bottom. Ashok and Riya pulled me out.

I was thoroughly drenched and felt chilled to my bones. I was wearing a pair of shorts, brown sandals, and a T-shirt. So, drenched as I was, we walked all the way home to 9 Highbury Gardens in Seven Kings. I clearly recall, whilst walking home, that I could see my sandals leaving footprints of water on the park's concrete footpath, one step at a time. Upon reaching home, Ashok and Riya were told off for not looking after me.

My father's younger sister Shanta Devi Bhardwaj had married Vidya Sagar in 1952 in Kitna, Punjab. Uncle Vidya Sager had travelled to London on 16th September 1961 from Nairobi. On his arrival he stayed with my father at 38 Princlet Street. He worked various jobs to earn money and in 1962 he ventured out to Bradford, Yorkshire. Uncle Vidya and Auntie Shanta along with their 6 children, travelled to London on 5th June 1965 from India and stayed for a few days with us at 9 Highbury Gardens. We shared sleeping arrangements with Uncle Varinder at 102 Pembroke Road, Seven Kings.

After that, they went to Bradford, where they settled and returned to London in 1969 and temporarily stayed with Uncle Naresh Chander, at 13 Lansdowne Road, Seven Kings, until they could secure their own home. On 10th January 1970, 13 Windsor Road was purchased from Uncle Joginder Sanger at the behest of my father. After a while, a grocery shop was established on Ilford Lane, and they traded as Kumar Bros.

They were five brothers: Satish, Ashok, Rajesh, Rakesh, Suresh, and one sister, Sushma. We always looked up to her as our sister. We called her sis; that was her nickname. We used to have a weekly feast she would cook for all the brothers at 13 Windsor Road, Ilford. That's when I became aware of all the different foods and recipes.

Sushma, my cousin sister was a Rajesh Khanna fan and collected posters and articles from Bollywood magazines, such as Picture post, Stardust, Movie, Cine Blitz and others. Once over a weekend stay, at their home at Windsor Road, Ilford which was regular occurrence, she showed us her collection of scrap books, very beautifully kept and arranged. They were her prized possession. As a ten year old, I was tempted to take one of her books quitely. I am sure she noticed subseqently, that one of the scrap books went missing. But she was too kind, to say anything. The love and respect we all shared was amazing. Many years later, on one of my milestone birthdays, she wrote in my birthday message book to me that she knew that I had taken her scrap book. For more than 50 years or so, she kept silent. That's sisterly love. The question now arises do I return the scrap book or keep it?

I had become close to one of the brothers, Rajesh Kumar aka Loom, and at the time, he used to study at Loxford High School at Loxford Lane, off South Park Drive. In the early 70s, I recall that area used to be an uncut and overgrown forest. It was a no-go part of Ilford. But it was developed, and a successful school Loxford High School was built along with new houses, shops, etc. The complete area was regenerated.

After school, once a week, we used to go swimming. I believe Rajesh was the one who taught us, i.e., Krishan and I, how to swim. At times Rajesh's classes would finish early, and we would still be at school, as our school ended at 3.15 pm – 3.30 pm. So, whoever arrived earlier would write a message with chalk on the footpath outside our home, at 9 Highbury Gardens. The message was meant to let the others know who had arrived first.

Our local swimming pool was on the High Road in Seven Kings. The Isaac Newton Academy now occupies that space. There used to be two pools: one bigger pool for the more experienced swimmers and the second for beginners. There was a canteen, and after swimming, we would buy our regular cheese roll, Coke, and Wagon Wheel biscuits. Those were fun times.

In the early 70s, another pass time was regular family trips to Southend in Essex, to the beach. In the summer months, usually on a Sunday, all families would prepare food and drink baskets and head to the beach. At times, there would be 20 or so of us in separate cars. Once there, we would pick a spot and pull out our blankets. We then had snacks like samosas, pakoras etc., on the beach. Our usual spot was in the hilly green area, looking out towards the sea. We would love the treats, ice cream, doughnuts, cotton candy, and peanut fudge. We used to ride the fairgrounds and I loved the bumper cars. That used to be our regular outing. The cool breeze from the sea was a delight and I used to look up into the blue sky and dream of the future.

In the early 1970s Ashok, my brother and I would dress Krishan, my younger brother up as a Guy Fawkes and put him in a pram and stand outside Seven Kings station and ask Penny for the Guy from the public. We continue to celebrate Guy Fawkes on 5th November with fireworks. It's strange how things you used to do when young, continue with you as you grow older. Where now stands The Seven Kings medical centre at Swindon Close, was barren land and small slopes of hills and overgrown pastures. We brothers would race in empty crates down the slopes and occasionally hurt ourselves with a rough and tumble. But we were strong kids and never let that bother us.

In those times, Ashok was a young rebel. Around the early 70s, one evening the front door was rammed open, and Ashok entered shouting, *"Quickly hide, and turn the lights off. They are after me."* Before we knew it, the house was pitch black. My mother ran into the passageway from the kitchen and wanted to know what was happening. Ashok explained that a group of kids was chasing him, and he feared they would beat him up. My mother sensed the danger and opened the front door. She picked up the nearest thing she saw, a milk bottle from the milk crate. With all her might, she threw the bottle at the howling kids, and they got the shock of their lives, seeing this woman coming at them hurling empty milk bottles. They ran a few feet and took cover behind our neighbour's front hedge. It was enough for the bullies to run for their lives. That's how my mother was, protective of her cubs. It goes without saying that Ashok was given a dressing down soon after and promised to behave. He was a rebel, without a cause.

My initial schooling was at South Park Infants School on Water Lane, Seven Kings. It was just minutes away from our grocery shop on Green Lane. I enjoyed school, particularly the sports lessons. I was always willing to please and stand out from the rest of the class. I was an average student at school, but my sports activities gave me much confidence and helped me make friends easily. At school, many Asians were isolated and kept to themselves at the time. School was fast becoming multi-cultural, with its mix of students.

I was chosen to play for the school football team, which was a great honour. I wore the number 10 shirt, after my hero, Pele of Brazil, and the school kit was a yellow jersey, blue shorts, and yellow and blue socks. Soon, I was outshining others on the team. Once, I recall that with minutes to go, I got a penalty and was asked to take it. It was a draw so far, and if I had scored, we would have won the game, and I would have become the team's hero. I placed the ball on the spot and took a few steps back, and as I ran and kicked the ball, it trickled slowly into the goalkeeper's hands. I messed up my penalty kick. It was a considerable embarrassment, and I did not know where to hide my face in shame. I felt humiliated for the first time on the football field. That was a crucial lesson to learn. Never take anything for granted.

Next door to our shop at Green Lane, Seven Kings was The Surplus Supplies Store, and they had another store in Goodmayes, where I would work and earn some extra money, run by Jack, Mary, and Martin Hughes. Ashok, Krishan, and I were asked to look after the store from time to time, while they went out to do deliveries, etc. They had a white till which would make a sound when the register was pressed open. We were good kids, and they trusted us. We became close friends with the Hughes family, especially with their son, Martin and he treated us like younger siblings. He was a smart young lad who had seen life. On the other hand, we were just about to experience this life as young boys.

He used to take us to the movies at ABC Ilford, which is now situated on the one-way system, where Prabha Banqueting is located, close to Ilford Police Station. We saw movies like The Italian Job, with Michael Caine, Herbie Rides Again, On the Buses series, What's Up Doc, and Doc Savage- The Man of Bronze, to name a few. It was a whole new experience for us young guys. We became more confident. Close to Southend in Essex, where they kept a speed boat, and during the summer, we would go and water ski. To be precise, Martin would water ski and Krishan, and I would swim around or pick up the skis if they fell off. We were introduced to Cracker Barrel Cheese wrapped in gold and red covering. Life was merry. We had no worries. Not a care in the world. Just carefree kids, having fun and enjoying the delights of life.

Christmas has always been a special time of the year. Having been born and educated in Ilford in the UK, I read and was bought up around Christianity. The teachings of Jesus have left a significant impact on me. Learning Religious Education at school was fulfilling and enjoyable, being one of my favourite subjects. Enjoying choir service and singing Hymns at the school assembly were noteworthy moments and ones I looked forward to attending. I would say that I knew more about Christianity than I did about Hinduism.

Christmas in The Kumar household is a major event each year. A ritual which I started when I was a young boy at Highbury Gardens in Seven Kings till date. Both Megha and Ektaa have actively carried the traditions forward. To describe our run up to Christmas, the season of goodwill for us starts after Thanksgiving in November. The Christmas decorations are taken out carefully, which would have been wrapped and placed in boxes and marked up. We have two trees, one for the front outside garden and one for the internal living room. The trees are decorated by the four of us, with Christmas Carols and songs played in the background and this usually takes 2-3 hours. All other decorations around the house are put up carefully and ultimately creating a Christmas Wonderland. We just love the feel-good factor of Christmas. In the good old days of Christmas cards, I would write cards to family and friends, and I would love to receive them as well. Sadly, we all live in a different age now of messaging via the phone. Its not the same thing, is it? I miss those days, when life was more simple and fun.

I loved to watch the movies on Jesus Christ, Ben Hur, The Bible, King of Kings and many more. These were so meaningful and emotional at times. They gave a good message of spiritualism and good values. The Christmas celebrations, the lights, the colourful decorations, and how can I forget that it would snow at times? Christmas seems incomplete without snow. It's a time for forgiveness and to renew family ties and understanding. Exchanging gifts, the feeling of giving, it all makes me feel so good. The joy of writing Christmas cards and counting one's cards received from family and friends. It's now all a thing of the past with the latest technology, whatsapp messaging service. In later years, I would put up a Christmas tree in the front garden, lit up with lights and decorations. William Torbitt Junior School is near by, the young kids and their parents would stop by and take pictures in front of the tree.

I love to listen to Gospel music, especially that of Elvis Presley. I have found that over the years it has been very calming and spiritual for me. My favourite gospel songs are How Great Thou Art, He Touched Me, His Hand in Mine, Let us Pray and so many more.

For Elvis Presley, Christmas was always his favourite time of the year, with Graceland in Memphis all lit up with colourful lights and a nativity area set up on the grounds. Our neighbour at No 7 Highbury Gardens, Jim, a tall English man, always visited on Christmas Day with presents. It was a stocking of chocolates for me and my two brothers, Ashok and Krishan. That was a highlight at Christmas we used to look forward to. Our neighbours at No 11 were The Jamonda family, and I occasionally spent time with their daughter Tina watching TV and playing games. I recall they kept an immaculate and tidy garden with plenty of green grass and colourful flowers. They had an aeroplane fixed on a tall wooden pole in the rear garden, I recall.

Dad and Mum @ Highbury Gardens Ilford Essex 1963

Raj, Suresh, Mum Summer 1963

Raj, Suresh, Dad 1965

Suresh aged 3 with Dad in 1966

Krishan, Big B Raj & Suresh 1965

Suresh, Krishan & Ashok @ Highbury Gardens Ilford 1968

Krishan & Suresh at Photo Studio at Seven Kings Road 1965

Suresh aged 10

Bhaji, Dad, Krishan & Suresh in Apra Punjab 1969

Class of Mrs Tyler @ South Park Junior School 1975

Michael Ball, Suresh, George Quartey, Ayo Nicholls,
John Hunte @ Seven Kings High School 1978

Suresh & Friends Seven Kings High School 1978

Chapter 3

Growing Up - The Sporting Years

South Park Infants School in Water Lane Seven Kings… my first school. I have vivid memories of my mother walking me to school on the first day. I was very nervous because the first day of school meant that I would be meeting many new people. I was anxious, quiet and shy. One might say I was experiencing social anxiety, particularly because there were not many Asian kids around in those days.

I wondered, *'Would I make friends? Was I going to be picked on?'* I headed to school with uneasy thoughts racing through my mind despite all these fears. However, my fears only lasted till the first day.

Next to the South Park Infants School site was the South Park Junior School. Soon, I developed a lot of confidence and was even selected to play in the school Football team and participate in all other sports. Our playing ground was called Knox Field, based on South Park Drive, and it was within walking distance from the school. I would look forward to all sports activities with much enthusiasm. I thoroughly enjoyed sports and felt that I improved my game each week.

One Christmas on my way to South Park Junior School, I found some loose change strewn on the road and used it to buy some glitter bottles and decorations from the corner shop on the junction of Homefield Road and Green Lane. I showed it off and decided to give most of it to school friends. I got a lot of attention, and it felt good. In those days, it would have been worth around £2. For some of my fellow students, Christmas would have seemed to have come early.

A few days passed uneventfully. Then came the time of reckoning. The Headmaster, Mr Brown, called me to his office and ask where I had got all this money. He wondered if my parents were aware of it. So, he went to my mother at the shop and asked her. But, of course, she was not aware of this sudden windfall. That afternoon, the school teacher gathered all the glitter gifts from all the pupils and put them in a box. Most of it had been either used or thrown at each other; you know, stuff that young kids do.

I was mortified beyond all imagination. All these gifts I had given out were now being collected and handed in. I could not face my friends and hid for the next few days until calm was restored. My philosophy was that if I kept myself out of sight, the incident would soon be wiped out of my friends' memories. I am not quite sure how well that philosophy worked. Perhaps some of my classmates still remember me as the kid who found money to buy them all gifts.

This incident was a public embarrassment, and it felt awful. However, I learned a very important lesson that day; never take money that is not yours. Also, never show off and always stay humble. These lessons have remained with me throughout my life.

Watching T.V. was one of my hobbies. A serial called The Saint, starring Roger Moore, was very popular in those days. I would visit my friend's place at 1, Leamington Gardens, Seven Kings, to watch it on their colour TV. At the time, my best friend was Gary Zucconi. His mother really looked after me. She introduced me to peanut butter sandwiches. I became close to the Zucconi Family. Gary's mother Vera, and dad Jack.

One Christmas, during the annual Christmas School play, Gary and I designed white-boxed Robot costumes. The costumes were a big hit, and we totally stole the show.

During this period at school, we used to have line dancing in the rear playground (situated behind the school) in the afternoon. Dancing with the girls was fun. I developed a crush on some girls. To honour and respect them, I opt not to mention their names here. I was no different from any other red-blooded young boy.

Around this time, I met Tony Douglas, aka Philip Douglas, whose family used to live at Elmstead Road, Seven Kings. They were around the corner from our grocery shop K.B. Foods, on Green Lane. The Douglas family was a large family and rough around the edges. The kids were naughty and nice. Philip was the mild one, gentle and sweet.

At the Surplus Supplies store in Goodmayes, I came across all sorts of people from different backgrounds. I had many different experiences and faced various situations in quite a short period. I learned a lot by speaking to people and watching how Jack and Martin sold goods. I observed the negotiations that went on and business was conducted. These experiences all came in handy in the future.

Every Saturday, I was paid £0.50p and any tips or loose change that came my way. After a year or so, I saved £28 in a blue piggy-looking saving bank given to me by my father. The piggy bank was kept in my dad's room for safekeeping.

During lunch hour, I used to go across the road to the cafe, and it was here that my tastes began to develop. I would have a sausage sandwich, sausage roll, or bacon roll with ketchup. At teatime, I would have biscuits and hot chocolate. My taste buds were developing.

It was hard work, especially during the winter months, but I never missed a Saturday. Occasionally, if I had a Saturday morning football match, I was allowed to go and return afterwards. My goal was to save enough money and purchase my dream Rayleigh Chopper Bicycle, which was priced around £33.95 at Halfords at Cranbrook Road, Ilford. On 26th May 1973, after much thought, my father and I took a number 25 bus to Halfords. I was short and asked dad to contribute the remaining amount, of £6. We purchased the new bicycle with a padlock. The total came to £33.95. They did not deliver, and we had no van. So, we took a black cab back home to Highbury Gardens. The red and yellow Chopper bike was coming home in style. It was another dream come true, yet again. One more wish ticked off my bucket list. I have always felt that I have had the hand of God on my shoulders and that I could do anything that I put my mind to.

The bike was my prized possession, and I had a great time riding with friends. A fellow Chelsea FC supporter, Bob Whitehall, a friend from South Park School, already had a blue Chopper. These Chopper bikes were a craze in the early 1970s.

The early 70s were a time of fun and games. I was studying at South Park Junior School, and during the autumn season, us friends used to go picking conquers from fields. I recall one incident at the Canon Palmer School site on Benton Road, when in 1973, it was just barren land and a small forest with trees and scrubs. It was a good place to pick some conkers.

So, I and my friends Gary Zucconi and Rob Whitehall went to look at the site after school. The idea was to throw a big log of wood into the tree and thus make the conker batches fall to the ground. It worked fine for around 30 minutes or so.

One time, Gary had thrown a log into the tree, and I was still underneath it, collecting the conkers from the ground that had fallen a few minutes earlier. The log of wood brought down the conkers and, at the same time, hit me squarely in the middle on the top of my head. I fell to the ground, with a stream of blood coming from my head and a gush to show. Our home at Highbury Gardens was barely 5 minutes away. I was 11 years old. The boys had decided to call it a day and took me home. Krishan and Ashok were worried. Out came the first aid box and they could not find any band-aids. But instead, they put sellotape on the wound to stop the blood from oozing down my face. Unfortunately, the blood kept trickling down.

Dad was awoken by all the commotion. He was rather upset, but we kept quiet and did not tell him. As he sat down with us at the dining room table while having tea, he saw a trickle of blood drip into my tea. He was not pleased, to say the least. Dad had a night shift to attend at Ford.

It was around 7.30 pm, and the situation was complicated. Rather than call an ambulance, Ashok, Krishan, dad, and I walked to King George Hospital A & E Department on Eastern Avenue, Newbury Park. As we walked, I could see droplets of blood staining the pavement after each step. For the entirety of that walk to the hospital, dad kept muttering abusive words under his breath.

By the time we reached King George Hospital, it was around 8:15 pm, and dad had to report for the night shift at 10 pm. I got five stitches in my head. Then dad walked us back home rather than calling a cab or asking for a lift. I had a throbbing headache and was in no condition to walk. But somehow, I managed, and we made it home. As we walked back, following the same route we had taken to get to the hospital, we could see the blood-dried droplets on the footpath.

All this time, mum was at the grocery shop and did not know what had transpired until we got home and told her. I still have a small scar on the top of my head, which reminds me of that day.

Since my dad didn't drive, a friend used to pick him up from our house for the night shift.

My early thoughts go back to the early 70s when we watched The Big Match hosted by Brian Moore on Sunday at 2 pm just after the Thunderbirds TV series and Match of the Day hosted by Jimmy Hill on a Saturday evening. These football programmes were a must, and I would watch the players closely, studying their style and conduct on the football pitch. Some of my football heroes were Pele of Brazil, Chelsea stars of the 1970s Peter Bonetti, Peter Osgood, Ray Hutchinson, who had the long throw, Alan Hudson, Ron Harris, West Ham stars Bobby Moore, Sir

Geoff Hurst, Frank Lampard, QPRs Stan Bowles, Gerry Francis, Dave Thomas, Liverpool's Kevin Keegan, Steve Highway, Graeme Souness and many more…

Another favourite TV show of mine was Michael Landon's Little House on the Prairie and Highway to Heaven. He made his debut in Rawhide a western TV series. He made meaningful storylines with a message of hope for society. I would tear up watching some of these stories on TV. These were big influences in my growing up and progressive life.

I had a great affinity for my class teacher, Mrs Britton, and her husband, who taught us P.E. Mrs Tyler, my form teacher in the 4th year at South Park, was one of my favourites. I owe her a lot of credit for encouraging me to do well at school. My English really improved during this time. Prior to her efforts, I used to have an Indian accent and spoke funny.

I felt my confidence soar each year at school. I observed that other Asian kids were ignored or picked upon, whereas I always ran with the popular kids and made many friends. I was never bullied at school. I found it easy to make friends and always admired the girls! The fact that I was a talented sportsman helped me keep my chin up.

Due to geographical and boundary changes, moving into senior school at Seven Kings High School saw many of my friends going to Mayfield High School. I parted ways with friends such as Gary Zucconi, Robert Whitehall, Mark Howell, and many more. However, Philip and I went off to Seven Kings High School on Meads Lane, Seven Kings. Here I once again excelled at sports and became School Captain. I was fortunate to have good P.E. teachers, like Keith Thunder, Mr Kingdom, and Mr Harrison, who also taught Geography and English, and Mr Williams, who taught Geography. Mr Patterson was our music teacher. Mr Crisp, our history teacher was a delight.

I was not very strong academically and was considered an average student. However, the fact that I excelled at sports always made up for it and won me respect. Unfortunately, those three years at the school at the lower site passed very quickly.

Beal Grammar for Girls at Charter Avenue, Ilford, Essex, became Seven Kings High School's upper site and a secondary school. The Headmistress was Mrs MB Evans, and I enjoyed learning during these years. Mr Colin Gratrix was our Chemistry teacher. He renovated his house at Lambourne Gardens, Seven Kings, not too far when where we lived and at times I would go and assist him with work. This is where I found my DIY habit, really enjoyed the experience and learnt many valuable skills that would help me in future years.

In the 70s, I listened to the radio regularly, especially during my working Saturday and that's where my love for different genres of music was born, and I absorbed a lot of the music I was exposed to. I recall Neil Diamond's classic song, 'Song Sung Blue.' It was played regularly on the radio as well as Elvis Presley hits. 'Seasons in the Sun' by Terry Jacks. 'Honey' by Bobby Goldsboro. 'What a wonderful' world by Louis Armstrong and many more… I was open to all kinds of music and thoroughly enjoyed it. But my all-time favourite was and still is The King, Elvis Presley.

To earn extra income, I worked washing dishes on Saturday evenings for a short time at The Corinthian Restaurant on Eastern Avenue at Gants Hill.

I was fortunate to have close friends at Seven Kings High School, John Hunte, George Quartey, Chris Johnson, Mark Cumberworth, Lesley Williams, Hazel Cox, Alison O Shea, Gail Srivener, Joanne O Callaghan, Deanne Christopher and many more, and a Rock N Roll follower Ray Lambert, who stayed at Norfolk Road, Seven Kings, close by and he also loved Elvis and we would meet up and listen to Elvis records on an old style turn table record player.

One day after school, whilst some of us friends en route to home, walking down St Johns Road in Seven Kings, off Aldborough Road South and Stainsforth Road, a car screeched by us with two men, who jumped out and came towards us. All the friends did a runner, and they were fast, but John Hunte for some reason was caught off guard and was slow to react. He was circled by these men, and I stopped and looked back and saw this and ran back towards John to assist and support him. This was going to get messy, I thought to myself, and I could leave my friend on his own, but it was fine, no blood spilt. We were advised that they were Police officers in plain clothes and were looking for someone, and they thought we may have been the kids they were looking for. It ended amicably with goodbyes and apologies from the Police officers. Later we all had a good laugh over the incident.

I had raised my game in football and had been noticed for my football skills. I felt honoured when I was approached to play for clubs.

Up until Seven Kings High School, Philip and I trod the same path regarding schooling. We frequently played football together, due to which I came to know he was quite a sportsman. We stayed in touch even after school. His father-in-law, Alan, occasionally assisted him in the family business, i.e., building and decorating. Over the years, he had even done some work for me.

Once, I recall, we were playing the Seven Kings High School 5th year Football team, and we were in the 4th year. It was a rivalry game of football. The goalkeeper kicked the ball up the field towards the halfway line, and Philip volleyed the ball right back into their goal. It was a classic goal.

With a grieving heart, I share the news that Philip passed during his building days due to asbestos poisoning. I got to know about his death through Facebook and was very saddened at the loss of such a good friend.

I recall during this rival match between the two years, 4th and 5th, at Seven Kings High, Ronnie Hard Man Fursey tried to take me out of the game with a crushing tackle. He nearly broke my leg. I was in pain and was taken off and needed a week to recover. That's what certain games meant to people. Of course, there was a competitive side to the game. A blatant win-or-lose scenario. But these incidents made me a better and tougher player on the field.

During the summer holidays, there was an annual funfair at Valentines Park, Melbourne fields. Within it was a 5A Side football tournament, where local kids could participate and showcase their talent. I mustered up a team and won it for three years, in a row.

During one of the tournaments, a man named Arthur spotted me for my talent. He was an ageing man with a walking stick. He was a sort of scout, on the lookout for young talent. He came over, and we started to talk. He invited me to join West Ham Football Club. He connected me with Joe Lewis, the Manager for a local side called Old Fairlopians, based at Fairlop, Barkingside, and Essex. This was a senior men's team, and he wanted me to play for them. I felt grateful for the opportunity and thought it would help me get some valuable experience. Now I was playing football with the men and, boy, did I learn quickly! Some of these guys did not like Asians or Indians and played like animals. They played to break one's leg, all over a football game. The first year was tough, hard training and plenty of kicks and bruises to show. But I must say, the experience was invaluable. They would hurl abuse at me, calling me all sorts of names and trying to obstruct my game. My team members would rally around and support me.

It was 1976, I made some friends during my term with The Old Fairlopians. Mick Hurley, Neal Levy (he was the Captain), David O Mahoney, Joe Oxby, Rob Shepard, Steve Leak, Dave Madden, and others were talented players. These guys were some of the bests in our region. I was really enjoying football. I was lean, fit, and the best at my game. I was voted Player of the Year in my first year at a celebration at Nans Pantry, situated at Eastern Avenue, Newbury Park. I was honoured to be presented the trophy by England's Legendary Cricket batsman, Graeme Gooch. It was the highlight of my career.

I had won several medals and trophies by now, but this was the best so far. The trophy was a prized treasure for me. Seeing my name engraved on the cup was a moment of great pride for me. It rested on my mantelpiece at home for several years. I still have it as memorabilia from my sporting days. My parents and family were very proud of me. It was a great feeling of accomplishment.

I had all my medals displayed on a mantelpiece in my bedroom at 69 Norfolk Road, Seven Kings, and at a celebration at home, a young cousin sneaked in and stole some of my medals. Some were never found. Of course, I was angry, but the cousin was just a young kid. I did give him a few slaps, though, because I really cherished my medals and trophies.

The local press, such as Ilford Recorder, covered these matches. Ironically, they never seemed to get my name right. I was often referred to as Sukh Mohammed, Shooki, Suki, etc., but I believe my talent did all the talking on the pitch. So, I didn't take it to heart that they were misspelling my name.

I scored some great goals and had the best time of my playing career during this time. But unfortunately, there was still no money coming my way. The occasional drink, sandwich, or fish and chips were all I got for my weekly efforts.

In 1978, while at Seven Kings High School, I was offered an apprenticeship to teach, by my P.E. teacher, Mr Keith Thunder, who was one of my favourites and was liked by all, because of his easy going nature and appeal. He was always very supportive and offered encouragement and spent a lot of his time guiding me. I was keen to take it as I did not wish to be recruited into the family travel business. I was adamant, and my family knew that I wanted to stand on my own feet and be independent. My senior 5th form at Seven Kings was ending, and I wanted to go on to the 6th form and teach P.E. Unfortunately, my mother had other ideas. I loved my mother, so I compromised. I agreed to try out the family business in the summer of 1979. I commenced work for my brother Satish at Union Travel situated at 93, Piccadilly. During that summer, I got my first taste of the business world. Oh, did I like the sweet smell of power and authority!

Ashok, Krishan, and I used to play football on the street, outside our home at 9 Highbury Gardens. Krishan was a keen goalkeeper, his idol was Liverpool's Ray Clemence and Ashok and I used to take potshots at him, standing in the front yard brick wall, which was used as a goal. Cars would come and go. The sound of horns was a constant. We would play late into the night. This went on for many years. Several times, Krishan would miss the ball, it would break the glass and go into the front room. Naturally, this resulted in plenty of scolding from the family.

As more and more cousins moved closer, it became a ritual for all the boys to play football each Sunday afternoon, mainly at Seven Kings Park, off Meads Lane, Seven Kings. Loxford Park in Ilford was another regular location. My brother, Krishan, had developed into a first-class goalkeeper.

Our cousin, Ashok Sagar, hardworking, full of kindness and a calm guy, had a blue Volkswagen van, and he would one by one pick up all the team players from their homes on Sunday.

My family always encouraged me, and my brothers were supportive. They never got to play at that level themselves, I suppose. So, they wanted me to have the opportunities that they did not have. But they never had the time to watch any of my football matches.

I was fast becoming an all-round sportsman. Cross country, athletics, basketball... George Quartey, a school friend, from Seven Kings High was an amazing true talent at the game. We enjoyed cricket as well. I held the record at Seven Kings High in 1977 athletics for the fastest 400 metres in 61 seconds and 800 metres in 2 min 33.2 sec. I excelled at Cross Country running that year.

I played and enjoyed watching Tennis, my favourites were Ilie Nastase of Romanian, Bjorn Borg of Sweden, John McEnroe, Chris Evert of the USA, Evonne Goolagong of Australia, and our very own British Virginia Wade, who won the Ladies Wimbledon title of 1977.

Summer of 1979, the question was would I stay on to teach P.E. at Seven Kings High School, or would I join the family business? My football and sports career ended abruptly, no one was to blame but me. The business bug had bitten me somewhat. I just became intoxicated with business.

South Park Junior School Football Team 1973 with Head P J Drew

The Redbridge Football Team 1975

Redbridge & Essex Football Team 1976

Fairlop Football Team 1978

Fairlop Football Team 1977

Fairlop Football Club in Barkingside 1978

The Fairlop Football Team 1978

Old Fairlopians Football Team 1979

Chris Johnson & Suresh with Player of the Year Trophy 1979

Sports Day Seven Kings High School in 1978

Old Fairlopians Football Team 1978

Suresh with FA Cup @ The Emirates Stadium

Chapter 4

Come Fly with Me

London, 1954. These were tough times. My father, Pandit Kul Bhushan, migrated from his village Kitna (in district Horshipur, Punjab) to London. He wanted a better life for his family. *Till when will we live a life of poverty and face the lack of opportunities?* He felt it was his duty to provide his family with the best and that moving abroad was the most viable option. So, he set off with a small amount of money, leaving behind his father, Pandit Kali Sharan, his wife, Indra Sharma, and three young children. 7-year-old Raj was the eldest, followed by 4-year-old Surinder and 2-year-old Satish.

Leaving one's family behind in order to progress is no easy feat. It takes much courage to take such a bold step. But my father clenched his teeth and made a move to London. His eyes were filled with dreams while his heart ached to be home.

For five long years, my father strove day and night, working overtime to send money back home. My father was a warrior. Despite all the hardships he faced in London, he never gave up. He persevered and made more efforts to earn enough for us to live a comfortable life. He would keep very little for himself and would keep going. Perhaps the pint of Guinness that he swigged occasionally kept him going.

Our generation, as well as the ones that will follow, can never achieve the feat my father's generation managed to accomplish. Their generation had a lot of determination and courage. Our grandparents and parents were made from a different kind of material. Compassion and determination.

Gradually, he sponsored the rest of his family and helped them settle in London. His brothers, their families, and their children.

In 1961, Uncle Joginder Sanger came to settle in London. Initially, he was looking after a passport and immigration business for his brother, Roop Lal Sanger, who lived in Apra, Punjab, India. Our mother, Indra, was Joginder Sanger's elder sister, and my father's brother Varinder, was married to Joginder's younger sister, Prakash. So, there was a dual relationship in our households.

In those early days of settlement, working in a factory was a common means of earning some money, very few qualifications were required. But it was laborious work. Money was not great, but one got along.

Every weekend, family get-togethers were a must. Our mother and Uncle Joginder were very close, and he would look to her for guidance and support. Our mother treated everyone fairly and was very kind and generous. She had won everyone's respect by always giving sound genuine advice and being honest.

Some family members who immigrated from India stayed at our place until they figured out a place of their own. The first house that we all rented was at Broomhill Road, in Goodmayes, Ilford. It was a triple-fronted home jointly let by the families and a third party. This was fast becoming small for all the families. All agreed that time was right for all to purchase separate homes, for each growing family.

In 1963 we moved into our new home at 9 Highbury Gardens. Moving into a new house is always exciting. The family shared good vibes as all our relatives supported each other. The house at Highbury Gardens was purchased for £2200. A mortgage was secured from Natwest Bank, High Road Seven Kings. Our cousin, Om Prakash Kalia, contributed £125, as we were short on the deposit and subsequently reimbursed. A lifelong favour that Raj has never forgotten, and in later life, always looked after him and had a close relationship with O.P. Kalia.

Sometimes there would be 25-30 people in the house. We believed in the adage, *"The more, the merrier."* Mum and other ladies would be in overdrive in the kitchen, ensuring that all were well-fed. No one was allowed to leave without having had a hearty meal. This shows our culture of sharing and caring. The atmosphere was electric; card games and a trip across the High Road to the Cauliflower Pub were part of the routine. The bar staff would get busy as an order for 25 pints came in. We kids would run around the car park at the Cauliflower while red ale, cheese, and onion crisps would be sneaked out of the pub door to us by the elders.

In 1963, my father was working at Ford, and he became seriously ill and had tuberculosis – TB. He spent close to 10 months at St Andrews Hospital in Bow, close to Stratford. My mother would visit him daily, travelling by bus and making sure that he had enough home-cooked food. Ford arranged a collection for dad and the family, which was much appreciated. This was a custom, in those days, if any colleague was ill or off work for a long period. Friends and colleagues would make sure that the family was being looked after and they would call and visit as well on a regular basis. This was close to the time that Highbury Gardens was purchased and a Bow Hospital worker that my father became friendly with, Mr Hussain, kindly loaned £200 towards the purchase of the house. Once my father was discharged from the hospital, he made sure the money was returned with heartfelt thanks.

Eastways Travel was established in 1967 and run by Uncle Joginder. With the expansion of the business, uncle required support at the office in Brick Lane and asked his sister, Indra, if Satish could assist him in the office. Satish would work on the weekends since he was still attending school. The good thing about our family was that they would keep youngsters engaged in positive activities. In Satish's case, he was set up to gain experience by working at the office.

Around this time, Raj worked at the Lacrinoid Ship Carbon factory. Tony was involved in full-time education. In 1970, Raj also joined Eastways Travel and was out and about doing deals and making contacts, while Satish was running the office on a day-to-day basis and looking after the accounts. These boys made a good team, and the business flourished due to their hard work.

As a seven-year-old, I enjoyed accompanying my brother Satish on Sundays as he worked at Eastways Travel. We would catch a British Rail train from Seven Kings Station. Raj would mostly be out and about, going from agency to agency, collecting tickets, mainly based at the Regent Street office. That's where we all started, as these were the early stages of learning the craft. It is always a good idea to engage youngsters in business. Not only do you get a new perspective, but you also keep the young ones out of trouble.

With the growth of the business came a set of new complications. Misunderstandings over small things developed. Often, these misunderstandings were exacerbated by third parties, who would try to create issues and take advantage of the situation. The elders were no different to any other family.

In 1970, dad was well established at Ford, and mum was running a grocery shop at Green Lane, Seven Kings, Ilford. Tony was helping in the shop, buying goods, and doing deliveries. After doing a full day at Ford, dad would drop off at the shop and assist with the bookkeeping. The family was giving in all they could and trying to earn money. It was tough, but in retrospect, I believe we enjoyed that phase of our life. Working for a mutual purpose helps keep the family tied together and renews family bonds. We were lucky to have each other's support.

All our hard work seemed to pay off because our living standards improved daily. Raj, leaving school and joining the factory at the tender age of 15, was the need of the hour as we needed the money to run the household, there were bills to be paid, and dad's salary was not enough.

Eventually, in 1972, Raj and Satish set up their own travel office. It was called New Ways Travel and was situated on Edgware Road, Lon W2 and was successful. They commenced operations in the second office in Swallow Street in Piccadilly in 1973 which became a branch office for New Ways Travel. This office belonged to Ajit Jouhal, who was one of the early pioneers promoting travel to the Indian subcontinent. He was running Ranjit Travels and had the agency for Syrian Arab Airlines and Kuwait Airways. He had a lot of respect for our father and promised him the office. Ajit was a man of his word. Things were looking up, and the local ethnic community of East London was being serviced well by New Ways Travel.

My brother Tony was tough and joined the Air Cadets in Horns Road, Ilford. There he was taught self-discipline, studied about aircrafts and achieved a private flying pilot's licence. By 1973, Tony had completed his studies at Queen Marys College in East London and achieved a degree in Mechanical Engineering after a three-year course. Then he joined New Ways on Edgware Road to assist the growing business. Raj and Satish were stationed in Swallow Street. Dad had left Ford and was now looking after the accounts for the business and the day-to-day banking. He was disciplined, diligent and well-organised.

The family home at Highbury Gardens was becoming small as the family was growing, so Raj decided to move. He moved to a 3-bedroom house in Grosvenor Road, Ilford. The family home was now too small to accommodate all the new additions. Times were changing, and our mother was slightly uncomfortable with these changes. She wanted her flock to be together and remain close-knit. Every mother wants to see her nest full and happy. But as life progresses, the young ones take their flight. Family meant the world to her, and she wanted everyone to live in harmony. Business activity was always a hot topic of discussion in the family dining room.

Pan Am wanted to compete with Air India to the Indian subcontinent and looked at the market to appoint a General Sales Agent – G.S.A. An Agency with monopoly to sell the Airlines tickets to others, sub-agents and customers in the given territory.

In 1973, Pan Americans management in the UK, Don Mucullock, Director UK and Bob Wren, Manager UK saw how enthusiastic these young boys (my brothers) were. He acknowledged their hard work in travel and wanted to give them an opportunity to represent and work with Pan Am. Our parents were proud yet humble that the brothers had been blessed with a Pan Am GSA in the UK. All the hard work had paid off, and they were on the way to making money.

In 1973 Air India decided to appoint a GSA for the UK and Uncle Joginder managed to secure the appointment and established Hindustan Travel Service and became a market leader to India.

In 1973 our first cousins, O.P. Kalia and his brothers, Tarsem, Paramjit, Gopal and Keshav, opened Sam Travel at 805 Romford Road, along with their father Bagwant Kalia, our father and Raj helped them establish this office. They were given much support and credit facilities to help them get off the ground. They were to support Pan Am sales in East London and did so in the early years.

Raj left New Ways and established United Air Travel in Leicester Square in 1974. By now, Raj has managed to secure a GSA for Syrian Arab Airlines in the UK. He and Mr Pervez Khan became 50% partners, and United Air Travel was formed. It all worked out well, for everyone in the end.

Satish and Tony made some inroads and were keen to secure the GSA for the family. In 1975, the family was awarded The Pan American Airways - General Sales Agency for India and Empire Travel was opened, and thus began the relationship with Pan Am GSA in Southall. We had rented the offices of an existing Travel Agency, Nagra Travels at 35 South Road, Southall, Middx.

The business was reaching new heights and was very progressive during this time.

In 1976, Satish took the step to move out of Highbury Gardens. Everyone was upset and tried to convince him to stay. But his mind was made up, and he was moving on in his life. He moved to a one-bed flat in Acton, West London.

On the other hand, the same year, due to our sterling performance in London, Pan Am wished that we open an office in Frankfurt, Germany. So, Tony was sent to Germany to set up the business. New Ways Travel Frankfurt was opened on 2nd October 1976. He received support and guidance from Bill Bajpai, who was already running an established Travel Agency. Bill was a family friend and later became family when his daughter Sharmila married my younger brother Krishan. They were married at The Hilton Hotel on Park Lane. It was the first traditional Indian wedding with a small fire per Hindu traditions. I recall we were instructed to keep two fire extinguishers ready, in case the fire went out of control. But all went well. These were the early days of Indian weddings in Luxury Hotels and are soon to be capitalised by the Madhu's of Southall. Dad was now looking after Empire Travel in Southall, and he used to travel by train daily from Newbury Park Station to Southall, a journey that would take about one and a half to two hours each way.

He used to stop off en route to Piccadilly, drop off ticket stocks, etc. I recall one incident that he told me, wherein one evening he was returning late from Southall and was now on the Central Line from Holborn, headed for Newbury Park. For no apparent reason, some English-looking man stomped on this foot and walked away. Was this racism? I suppose, what else? My father was so shocked that he just froze and did not know how to react to the incident. When I started driving, I used to pick him up from Newbury Park Station, and when he limped to the car, he told me what had happened. He was in much pain, and I just wanted to go back and sort this guy out.

Satish was looking after the travel business in London with dad and Ashok. Raj was in full flight with Syrian Air, and by now, he was taking on new contracts with other airlines. His business was also growing fast. Tony was in Frankfurt.

In 1976, Norfolk Road, a triple-front home in Seven Kings, was purchased for £16,500 for the family. The family was growing, and the young ones were growing fast and needed more room.

1977, Raj purchased a mansion at 30 The Drive, Southwood Ford Lon E18 for £70,000, a grand property. When our mother saw the house for the first time she asked Raj, can you afford this property, do you have enough money. Raj calmly reassured her and said all is well. The following Sunday, the whole family went to view it, and it was just amazing. All of us were thrilled with Raj's success and fortune.

We were focused on establishing Pan Am with minimum profit margins. We were in direct business competition with Air India. However, in terms of business, we were competing with Air India. This meant that we were working on smaller margins. We were on the standard 12% and giving 10% away to our sub-agents to increase sales for Pan Am and compete with Air India at the same time.

In 1977, Satish established Union Travel at 93 Piccadilly. The office was purchased from Kailash Kohli of Travelfast, and he had an Aeroflot - Soviet Airlines Agency.

In 1979, Raj's partner, Pervaiz Khan, who worked in United Air Travel, suddenly died of a heart attack and his wife, Doris, was widowed overnight. However, she went on to run Mayflower Travel on Duke Street, in Mayfair.

In 1979, I joined Empire Travel in Southall to support my dad in running the business. I had never forgotten the incident on the train with my father and wanted him not to use the trains. I learnt to drive at an early age. Firstly, in an Audi, Ford Escort and then BMW 528i. I was able to remove an obstacle from my fathers' life, as he could not drive. The two of us would go to

Southall together daily. This made my father's life a little easier, given that I used to drive him back and forth.

Since an early age, I have always loved to see aeroplanes in the sky and the beauty of their flight. It is such a satisfying sight. This may have motivated me, and I decided to follow a path in the travel industry.

As growth continued, income was steady, but expenditure was rapidly increasing due to expansion. Sales became the focal point of the drive, and more airlines flying to India caused a split in market share. In 1980, New Ways Travel was opened on Soho Road in Birmingham, as Pan Am sales needed to be secured from The North of England. In June 1980, an East London office at 791 Romford Road was opened to push Pan Am sales. It was opened as a branch of Empire Travel.

In 1981, Empire Travel became Indra Travel, named after our beloved mother, who sadly passed away on 4th September 1981. The impact of this I cover extensively in the chapters ahead. I decided to name an office in her memory so that her name would live forever within the community. She was always eager to support people and especially the early settlers who came from India. I suppose it reminded her of her early days when she came to Britain.

With success comes challenges and tribulations and in the early 1980s, our offices at Munchener Str Frankfurt were raided by German authorities, led by Lufthansa. Lufthansa were arch rivals in Germany of Pan Am. The raid was perhaps conducted because of our success in Germany for Pan Am. There was an undercutting price war, and Pan Am was winning in terms of sales and passenger numbers. Tony and the staff were marched to the local police station. Ashok had been away from the office when the incident happened but reported it to the authorities later. Warrants had been issued. Tony's wife Punam, with little Tina, his daughter, aged 11, in tow, were frantically making calls for help to London. The authorities in Frankfurt were heavy-handed. Heather Weston (one of Raj's former managers at Sterling Travel) and I flew to Frankfurt the following day on Pan Am to take stock and secure bail and release. Subsequently, the staff was released, but Tony and Ashok were held in custody. Thanks to Mr Saleem Zaidi of BCCI Bank, bail was issued, and both were released after a few days in lockup. The sole reason behind the raid was political. An attempt to close down the competition and stop Pan Am sales in Germany. Sig Ruffert - Director of Germany, and Mr Beckers of Pan Am stood tall behind us in the hour of need and we had the full support of Pan Am.

Sales were at an all-time high in Frankfurt, Germany from October to December 1980, and we were having a bumper year and had broken all previous sales records for Pan Am. I was in Frankfurt with Tony and Ashok and then returned to Empire Travel. By now, the travel industry was undergoing drastic changes; competition and margins had become tight. So, to save on costs, we decided to move out of Southall in 1993 as Tony had taken a big office at Sabena House in Piccadilly and started his own Sun N Sands Travel outfit.

After that, we represented Pan Am in Germany, New Delhi, the USA, and Canada, and it was a successful business relationship. With our combined efforts as a family, we managed to forge Pan Am's entry into the Indian subcontinent and generated a large volume of business on its international network.

We were thankful that we had the support of so many friends over the years within Pan Am. It was an honour to work with each one of them. Don Mucullock, Bob Wren, Hank Auerbach, Jim Berwick, Albert Clogg, Stewart Robertson, Alan Weedon, Clive Walton, Tim Sands, Ray Croxsford, Jerry Murphy, Len Pearce, Jeff Wolfe, Richard Delderfield, Carole Lewis, Harinder Sidhu, and so many more to mention. I raise a glass to Pan American World Airways, and thank them for the memories.

In 1980, an unexpected proposition came to my brother Raj and the family was presented with an opportunity to work with

Air India as GSA for the UK, Germany, Northern India, USA, and Canada.

Raj was introduced to Roy Chowdhury by our family friend Bill Bajpai. Mr Chowdhry, with his powerful connections, helped us in securing the Air India contract. He was close to Sanjay Gandhi.

Sanjay Gandhi, the son of the ruling Prime Minister Indira Gandhi, was allegedly running the country's day-to-day affairs and had become very strong in the country. He was fearless and feared by all. Roy Chowdhury arranged a meeting with Sanjay Gandhi. Sanjay asked what was required, and Raj asked for the Air India GSA, which was agreed upon, and aides were called and instructed accordingly. Sanjay was keen that we get involved in the hotel industry of India. But we were not interested, as we had no experience running hotels. Sanjay was not one for turning, and he had given his word, which was final.

As destiny would prevail, on 23rd June 1980, at 08:10 am, Sanjay Gandhi, in his light glider, crashed near Safdarjung Airport in New Delhi and died on the spot. He was flying a new aircraft of the Delhi Flying Club, and while performing an aerobatic manoeuvre over his office, lost control and crashed. He was sometimes very reckless, but India had lost a great leader, one who would have made a difference. It is said that upon hearing the news, both Indira Gandhi, the mother, and Maneka Gandhi, Sanjay's wife, rushed to the scene of the crash at Safdarjung Airport. This was a tragic loss to India.

Anyhow, it was sort of a bittersweet moment. Never again would we come so close to securing the Air India GSA. One would have to wait till 2012 for me to have another crack at it.

Meanwhile, Air India's GSA in the UK was terminated in 1983. Vikram Kaul, the first cousin of Indira Gandhi and son of Minister Shelia Kaul, was sent to the UK as OSD – Officer on Special Duty and concluded the termination of the GSA, and the Minister for Civil Aviation at the time was Khursheed

Alam Khan, father of Salman Khursheed, former Member of Parliament, and Minister in the Congress Party in India. As a result, Air India decided to appoint a new GSA, Welcome Travel.

In 1984, Indira Gandhi was assassinated by her bodyguards at 1 Safdarjung Road, her residence. She was shot while coming out of her private office and into the gardens to meet visitors and The Press, a sad loss for India, leading to the Sikh riots in India. A tragic day in the history of India. Many lives were lost due to this madness.

Rajiv Gandhi, a pilot with Indian Airlines and a reluctant heir, was sworn in as Prime Minister of India in a rush. He wanted that the Golden Temple in Amritsar to be rebuilt to its former glory. He approached his friend Tejwant Singh owner of Skipper Construction Company, to rebuild it, and allegedly in return, he asked for the Air India GSA for the UK. No travel experience but was being offered an attractive Air India contract.

It is said that Tejwant Singh of Skipper Construction, who had some associates in London, Om Gulati, an Electronics shop owner from Tottenham Court Road, and a successful clothing businessman Lucky Paintal, also a non-travel agent. So, the three partnered and established an Air India GSA and named it Welcome Travel. They recruited Ray Hutchinson from Air India, who was the UK Sales Manager.

Uncle Joginder Sanger, moving forward with the times, went on to create a Hotel Empire, The Bentley, The Courthouse, The Washington Hotel, The Heston Hyde, etc,. His success story continues to this day. A hard-working businessman like no other. A God-gifted man with a sharp mind and personality. I enjoyed my many discussions with him over Chai and a sandwich discussing the days of yesterday and his long road to success.

We have been privileged to work with some of the top Air Indians - The Maharajah's best and most dedicated personnel, over the years. Vikram Kaul, Ashvini Sharma, K D Row, Ashish Mathur, Kailash Singh, Yogesh Mundwa, Tara Naidu, Anil

Maken, Mukesh Bhatia, Debashis Golder, during his tenure he reached new highs for Air India revenue from UK and Europe and happens to be a music lover and a very talented singer.

We currently work closely with Air India, amongst other Agents appointed by Air India. Air India gradually, over a period, ran into difficulty, mainly over expansion and without proper checks and accountability. The company was fast on the decline. Sadly, The Maharajah was going through turbulence and crosswinds. Loses were mounting, and the Government of India was injecting more and more money into Air India. It was fast becoming a White Elephant.

Pan Am's business model was also on the decline due to specific corporate decisions, especially the takeover of National Airlines, which proved disastrous for Pan Am.

Unexpected and out of the blue, horror-struck, shortly after 19:00 on 21st December 1988, while Pan Am Flight 103 was in flight over the Scottish town of Lockerbie, it was destroyed almost instantaneously by a bomb planted in the forward cargo area, 38 minutes after take-off. The plane was at 31,000 feet. This was a regularly scheduled Pan Am transatlantic flight from Frankfurt to Detroit via a stopover in London and another in New York City. The transatlantic leg of the route was operated by Clipper Maid of the Seas, a Boeing 747-121. 259 passengers on board, 16 crew members and 11 individuals on the ground also died. Significant portions of the aircraft, including the engines, also landed in the town of Lockerbie, and other important parts, including the flight deck and forward fuselage section, landed in the countryside to the east of the town.

On January 8th, 1991, Pan American World Airways filed for bankruptcy protection. This followed the loss of more than $2 billion after ongoing financial troubles that continued to escalate. Ultimately, it led to the closure of one of the most iconic brands in US aviation history. The lack of support from the US Government made it difficult for Pan Am to continue.

Pan Am essentially became reliant on high-priced foreign fuel. The increase in fuel prices added some $200 million to the company's cost sheet in the year after the embargo. The New York Times said that international travel also took a hit thanks to fare increases necessary to offset the rising costs of operations. On December 4th, 1991, Pan Am formally ceased operations after months of financial distress. Pan Am Flight 436 was the last to carry the airline's flag, flying from Bridgetown, Barbados, to Miami, Florida, on a Boeing 727. The airline brought a series of 'firsts' to the aviation industry. From the Boeing 707 and 747 to scheduled transatlantic service and Beatlemania, Pan Am pioneered numerous initiatives across the spectrum.

Such was the goodwill and respect for Pan American around the globe that even after its collapse, competing Airlines accepted Pan-Am tickets that had been issued to travellers across the world network. Even knowing that they may not be paid for the passage, as Pan Am had filed for bankruptcy.

Pan Am brought the first 747-100 into service on 22nd January 1970, heralding a new era in aviation. For many passengers, their first time on an aircraft was experienced on a Pan Am 747 flight. The jumbo brought long-haul wide-body travel to the world and made flying more affordable. In time, the iconic airline and the equally iconic jet would become synonymous with one another. As a result, we had to change our business model overnight.

In 1992, we were approached by Charles Reindorf, Director of Sales for Pan African Airways, flying to Banjul and Accra in Ghana and offered a GSA to sell their tickets. It seemed a good proposal at face value, but all was not well later. We agreed to give them £30,000 per flight twice weekly, and we would have exclusive rights to all ticket sales. But it came to light that Pan Af had other side deals with travel agents and what we believed to be an exclusive contract was a farce. Our sales were divided, and we never managed to recover monies from ticket sales. However, we were fast approaching the busy period from October –

December, where we would recover most of our investment from the low season.

But before that, we discovered that Pan Af was not paying their debts, and landing charges had accumulated at Stansted Airport. Fuel bills and airport handling charges were unpaid. Word was out in the market that all was not well with the airline; bookings stopped, and flights were cancelled. We lost a large sum of money.

We sued the Airline, but they were registered in Banjul, Gambia, with no tangible assets. It was a paper airline, as such. We obtained a High Court judgement, but there was no way to enforce it. So, we lost heavily but were duty-bound to return much of our client's monies which we had taken for flights, which were now not going to take off. There were ugly scenes in the office because passengers thought we were the Airline and not just the selling agent. They were chasing us for the monies paid to Pan Af. The airline offices in Bishops Stortford, Essex had closed overnight, and the staff quickly flew back to Banjul.

Pan Af had good potential, but there was too much interference from the shareholders, and the local management could not properly run the airline. It was an expensive lesson for us. It took close to one year to resolve the fallout from Pan Af. But we maintained our goodwill. Later, Charles Reindorf tried to start another Airline, but without much success. Times had moved on for us all.

1993 at Indra Travel, for some unknown reason, which remains a mystery, IATA made allegations of undercutting fares and, upon the evidence provided, this was to be proven incorrect. The revelation showed us that certain people targeted us within the travel industry. Our revenue with BA had increased rapidly, because Tony Newman, who was the general manager at Greaves Travel, named after the great Football legend Sir Jimmy Greaves of West Ham and England, had joined us, as a Sales Director. The owners of Greaves Travel were Russi Cambata, son Shahrookh

Cambata and daughter Mehra Dalton and the Cambata family over time had become the top sales agent for British Airways around the globe to the Indian subcontinent. Greaves Travel was a well run travel company, which had much support from within the industry. We share a close friendship.

Personalities in business, make all the difference, as we came to know and experience. In 1994 Barclays Bank withdrew its banking support from Indra Travel. The bank, for some months, had become nervous about the changing concept of low margins the business was returning. They had a change in policy about uncleared funds and withdrew its support and banking facility, thus resulting in the business collapsing. We received many payments in the form of cheques or credit cards from customers.

Monies were owed to Travel companies from whom we had purchased tickets. Combined with the IATA allegations and Barclays action, there was no option but to liquidate the company. There were customer monies due, and we managed to clear all commitments and over £100,000 debts were owed to our travel partners for flight tickets that we had purchased. Some were close friends, whom I had known since I started in travel, in the late 1970s.

I had some contacts at Natwest Bank at Ilford, and Mike Smith, the local Manager, was very supportive, and we managed to secure a loan. I arranged to pay off the debts of £100,000 owed and could continue to trade and have the support of the industry. I had built substantial goodwill over the year, and the companies were more than happy to wait for their monies. By the end of 30 days, all were paid and cleared, one by one. I could have walked away from the debts, but the right and honourable move was to make the payment and maintain one's reputation. I know, as a fact that many would have walked away and shrugged their shoulders and blamed the bank. That was not me, as I lived with a conscience daily.

In 1995, we re-established Indra Travel. It was time to build again, but we were sure it would be more difficult this time. Pan Am was no longer around to give us credibility. So, we were forced to buy tickets from other Consolidators and suppliers. Nonetheless, we marched on into the future after suffering a major setback.

The travel and aviation industry was changing and had become more competitive. Many more small operators were opening now and selling travel at lower prices with very little margins and overheads. Even early signs of Agents working from home and selling tickets, with very little overhead costs, were developing and spreading fast.

The GSAs and Monopoly days were fast behind us, and Airlines believed that the more Agents they had selling their tickets, the more business they would be able to secure. Not always the case, as with multiple agents comes low margins, and overheads begin to get higher. That caused agents to default on payments to Airlines, and during this period, many airlines had high debts that were unpaid by Travel Agents.

This was why I wanted to diversify and look at other ventures. We were comfortable and Indra Travel was on autopilot, and I had time to look at other subjects that I enjoyed. I was always interested in politics and wanted to make a difference for my local community and the country in that I had grown up. I felt that our family and I owed so much to Britain that I ought to do more and try to make a difference. It was time to give back to society and make a difference for the betterment of the community.

One of those new projects was the Punjabi Centre on Ley Street Ilford, a Community Centre and Sir Neil Thorne former Conservative Member of Parliament for Ilford South, had secured the site from Plessey's for the Punjabi community. Darshan Singh Mann, Sansar Singh Narwal, Dilbagh Singh Chahal along with others were the initial founding members and had done a lot of work to establish the Punjabi community in Redbridge. They worked tirelessly and gave much support. Many years later and at their request I accepted the position of Secretary at The Punjabi Centre. The youth were reluctant to get involved and I thought that I may be able to change this in time. I changed the format of events which were held and introduced more of Bollywood and dance numbers in the annual programmes. But as in any community project, there are people who will never accept change and stand in its way, thinking they know better. I served for a year or so and decided to move on but believe that I changed people's mindsets for the better and making the Punjabi Centre more inclusive and open. Some people have political agendas and love just to hold their positions and act like dinosaurs. These public institutes belong to all and no one or group of induvial has a right to dictate what should happen.

Pan Am You Can't Beat the Experience

Suresh @ Empire Travel Pan Am GSA Offices in Southall 1982

Don McCulloch Pan Am & Parshotham Lal Sharma

Chapter 5

When the Music stopped

Haridwar, one of the famous religious destinations of India is located at the foothills of the Himalayas with the holy river Ganges running through it. Haridwar has many temples and is the gateway to the main pilgrimage sites of Uttarakhand in India.

Each year, millions of Hindu pilgrims visit Haridwar to take a dip in the holy waters of the Ganges and participate in various religious rituals. As per the Hindu religion, bathing in the river Ganges absolves sins and helps with the purification of the soul, allowing it to access the liberation of "Nirvana". The water of river Ganga is considered so sacred at Haridwar, that pilgrims carry back the water from the Ganges.

Many tourists also visit this famous city in quest of peace and spirituality. The city welcomes its visitors with the chimes of the temple bells and the religious chanting of the priests. In fact, The Beatles, famous English pop group, toured Haridwar and Rishikesh (a place nearby) in 1968, for a spiritual reawakening through meditation. The trip proved to be one of their most creative periods and they wrote reportedly 48 songs, with most of them ending up on the White Album, released later that year. 'The Beatles Ashram' is situated in Rishikesh and is one of the main tourist attractions, that many visit.

Thousands of visitors come to Haridwar daily for blessings. Many come to perform the final rites of their loved ones who have passed on. More often they carry little urns containing the ashes of their loved ones after cremation. This ritual is known as 'Asthi Visarjan', meaning ashes immersion in the holy water. There are professional priests, known as 'Pandits' who help the grieving family to perform these rituals as per the Hindu religion. Asthi Visarjan ritual has significant importance for Hindus, as they believe that it helps the soul in attaining peace and salvation after demise.

These holy men known as 'Pandits' have the responsibility of upkeeping and maintaining the large ledgers, where births and deaths are recorded. These records date back to 1194 AD. In fact, in various parts of India, Pandits keep Hindu pilgrimage records, as well.

For centuries, Hindu ancestors who have visited Haridwar for any religious purposes also visit the Pandit in charge of their family registers and update the family's genealogical family tree with details of all marriages, births, and deaths in the extended joint family.

In present-day India, people visiting Haridwar are dumbfounded when Pandits unexpectedly step forward and invite them to come and update their very own ancestral genealogical family tree.

A visiting family member is required to personally sign the family genealogical register furnished by his or her family Pandit after updating it for future family visitors and generations to see and authenticate the updated entries. Friends and other family members accompanying on the visit may also be requested to sign as witnesses.

The ancient custom of keeping family genealogies is not well-known today to Indians settled abroad, NRIs known as Non-Resident Indians.

A fraction of present-day Hindu descendants are now Sikhs, Muslims, and even Christians. It is common for researchers to find details of two or even more than their past seven generations in these genealogy registers. Sadly, I visited Haridwar with my family in 1981 to perform the final rites of my beloved mother, Indra.

1980 was a great emotional upheaval. Our mother had fallen ill. Dr Cherry in Goodmayes was her doctor, and when she was not well, I would accompany her on doctor's visits. However, being a very strong lady, mum would prefer not to visit the doctor and instead take painkillers to prevent us from worrying about her. At times we were unaware of her pain and stress, as she had hidden them from us.

She was close to Prakash, her younger sister and wife of our father's brother Varinder. They stayed at 102 Pembroke Road, Seven Kings, and on one visit to her house, mum mentioned that she felt some lumps under her armpits. The sisters were close enough to talk about such matters. We were alerted, and Raj decided to engage the help of a friend, Dr Subash Gautam, from King George Hospital, for guidance.

Dr Gautam spoke to a specialist, Dr Noon, who diagnosed mum with gallbladder stones. We took his word as gospel. But unfortunately, even though we could have afforded the best medical care for mum at the time, we just relied on friends who were not exactly qualified to give adequate medical advice. At this time, Raj was also acquainted with Dr Pran Luthra, another Doctor from King George Hospital.

Mum was very worried, and even the thought of having anything serious was enough to frighten her. But no one in the family was talking about the seriousness of her illness and why she was unwell. This was a first-time experience; quite frankly, the elders were shell-shocked and did not know how to turn.

Around the same time, I accompanied Mum to Dr Cherry's clinic, a surgical clinic in Ilford. She was experiencing tooth pain and asked Dr Cherry to extract two of her wisdom teeth. It was very painful for her, and she had cotton swabs packed in her mouth to stop the bleeding. We walked all the way there from Highbury Gardens and walked back, just to save on the bus fare.

There was no need, just that mother always saved money. We could have taken a minicab. But the thinking of the time was to save and build for the children and the future.

Dad and the brothers were determined to expand the business. They would leave early and return late at night. Somehow everyone was so caught up in life that no one saw the signs or noticed how mum's health deteriorated. We should have done more during these days.

By 1973, the Grocery Shop in Green Lane had been sold, and mum was exhausted. She pushed herself hard, and her health suffered. To earn extra money, she worked on the sewing machine. We were six grown men and boys, and there was plenty of washing and cooking. She never complained and progressed forth and did not wish to bother her boys with any trouble.

All accepted the explanation that mum had gallbladder stones, and it was understood that medicine would dissolve the stones resulting in mum getting better. Later, the gallbladder stones were removed at KGH by Dr Noon, a consultant. However, mum continued to get weak and ill.

After a series of further tests, it was confirmed that mum had breast cancer and she would need radiation treatment and a mastectomy. It was suggested that it would be fine once the breast was removed, and she would need some time to recover and recuperate. We were advised that it was not serious. Dr Gautam was leading the medical diagnosis, and Dr Noon was criticised for a wrong diagnosis. We should have sued and held him to account, but it was not meant to be. The word cancer was like the plague. It was unsaid, and everyone was worried. Mum was very nervous and thought she would not survive despite the operation.

In December 1980, our mother feared the worst and wanted to meet her sons Tony and Ashok in Frankfurt, Germany. I was already there since October, and she thought to say farewell. After a week, mum, Tony's wife Punam, young Tina in her pram, and

I returned to London. It was snowing in Frankfurt and due to a technical fault, the Pan Am flight got cancelled and our tickets were endorsed onto Kuwait Airways.

It was to be her second operation. It was decided to go forth with the mastectomy of her right breast. I could see that she was very anxious, and the thought of her breast being removed was just another blow for her. Nevertheless, she remained defiant and put on a brave face.

We noticed that in her mind, she had accepted that she did not have long to live. During this period, Krishan and I spent many hours with her, by her side and making her comfortable. Unfortunately, after the operation, it was discovered that cancer had spread very quickly to her liver and stomach and was now in its final stages, there was no cure, and she was not going to survive.

The family was advised that there were very few chances of her making it, so we should ensure her comfort and cherish her time left. No second opinion was sought; I wonder why she had not been taken to the US for further tests. Simple, this was called being uneducated. It was a case of the blind following the blind. Unfortunately, we didn't make the right choices during these difficult times.

During the summer of 1981, Dr Raval, a friend of Satish's from Acton, described cancer to the family in simple terms. It all felt numb, and we were all in a state of shock. We all attempted to look happy when we were with her, but she knew that something was up, and she would pass.

By 1981, mum was in and out of the hospital and was undergoing chemotherapy, an attempt to stop the cancer from spreading. She would travel by bus for her appointments and without support. Her boys were too busy even to notice, in their business and she struggled on. I look back in sadness now and can't believe that she was not supported during this time when she most needed us by her side. She was just taken for granted and the assurance that mum will be fine, nothing could ever happen to her. She was our rock.

Mum's survival was limited to a few weeks; she was in decline and looking very pale. Then, slowly, we noticed that she seemed to be giving up her fight against cancer. Finally, on 2nd September 1981, Mum was to start another round of chemo at Barking Hospital. Raj had come to pick her up and take her to the hospital. On getting into the car, Raj's Rolls Royce, she said she wasn't sure if she was coming back home. That broke our hearts.

It was 2nd September 1981. I was at the hospital and did not wish to leave her side, so I decided to spend the night at the hospital looking after her and doing some office paperwork. On the night of 3rd September, she was in pain and was coughing a lot. I called out to the nurses. The end was near. An hour or so before her death, I saw the nurse had given mum a big blue tablet, and after that, she went downhill. I have no idea what that was.

It was early morning on the 4th of September 1981, when I was asked to call the family priest. I immediately rang Norfolk Road. Dad answered the phone, and I explained what was happening and that they should come quickly. So, dad rang Raj, and they came to the hospital together.

It was too late. They did not reach the hospital in time. Our mother passed at 5:15 am. During the last few minutes, she was in much pain and was gasping for breath. I was standing outside her room when the doctors were working on her. I believe they knew and just gave up and made the end peaceful for her. This was the first time that I saw and felt death. I was strong and faced it with all my being.

It felt unreal and as if it was happening to someone else, not us. Time seemed to have stopped, and everyone was in a state of shock. This was the first death of a loved one in our family.

Our mother was 49 years old when she passed. Our father, after that, was lost and never really recovered since my parents were so close to each other and spent their entire lives together. They lived for each other and their six children. They had never lived apart except when father was in London in 1954, until the family came to London in 1962.

Dad, Raj and Urmil arrived at the hospital at 5:30 am, but it was too late. Mum had passed. Dad was hysterical and in shock. He could not believe it. I explained to them what had just happened and how matters had unfolded during the night. The light of our family was no more, and the family would never be the same again. The ship's anchor was no more, and the seas would be rough in times to come.

After a while, we gathered all mum's belongings and headed home. That afternoon, Uncle Joginder and Auntie Sunita Sanger came to Norfolk Road. Krishan and I were in the kitchen, and they came close and hugged us both to console us. That meant a lot to me; we were just numb and could not understand how we would go on without her.

Preparations were underway for the funeral to be held at Manor Park Crematorium. Tony and Ashok were in Frankfurt, Germany and were asked to come urgently to London. Initially, they were not informed of her demise. When they arrived at Heathrow, only then were they told by Mohan Sagoo, our accountant at Empire Travel - Southall, about mum's passing. They were in disbelief and shock.

East London had never seen such a large funeral. The family, friends, public, people she knew and even some unknown crowds came and paid their respect from all over. It was a grand funeral; she was much loved, and people from all walks came to attend. She was a well-respected member of the community in Redbridge. She was self-taught, a strong and divine lady, who always looked out for others and stood tall when needed.

It was an emotional time to lose a parent. But at least we had our dad. I was 18 years old when we lost our mother. Forward to 1993, we lost our dad to cancer and had to relive the same harrowing experience all over again.

I, Mona and our two children Megha and Ektaa had left the family house in 1992 and moved to the flats above Indra Travel. The kids needed their own space. My father was spending more time in India. On his next visit to London in 1992, I regularly visited Norfolk Road to meet him and discuss certain issues. I knew him well, his likes and dislikes. Without him saying anything, I knew his habits and whatever he needed.

One Sunday afternoon, I became very emotional and could not accept the fact that my father was staying away from me and not with me at the flat. So, I asked Mona to ask him to visit, and he came along with Krishan to figure out why I was having such an unexpected breakdown. I wanted to be close to him, and I kept holding his hand. I was just not in control of myself. I had no control over my emotions for the first time in my life. I just kept weeping, saying that my father should not leave me. That day, we travelled back in time and talked about so many good moments, growing up etc. After about two hours, I composed myself, got a grip and calmed down. It was an out-of-body experience.

My father asked me to move back to Norfolk Road, as even he felt that we could not stay apart, but it was too late. Personally, I felt that I had to find the inner strength to deal with this episode. I have managed thus far, and it has never happened again. I had felt as though a cord had been cut.

My feelings for my father never changed. I loved him ever so much. I am what I am because of his teachings, his exemplary personality and his discipline in life.

In 1992 our business suffered from recession, and I was spending long hours and more time at work. I became deeply involved in business matters, which ultimately collapsed in 1994. All my funds went into saving the business. Unfortunately, it did not help, and all was lost.

By 1993, dad spent more time in New Delhi and in our village Kitna, Punjab. In Delhi, he had a farm and would cultivate the land and grow plants and flowers. He would harvest and see some small monies coming in from the sale. But it was not about money. He took great pleasure in this, and it kept his mind occupied and busy. He could never sit idle, he was always doing things.

Raj had purchased a place in South Delhi at Greater Kailash Part 2, near Savitri Cinema, where dad used to stay with Cousins, Brij Mohan and his wife, Raja. My elder brother Raj brought them from the village to Delhi.

During the summer of 1993 in Delhi, there was an all-time heatwave, and it was very hot, even for dad. It was July now. One day at the farm, dad felt dizzy and felt like maybe he had sunstroke from the heatwave. So Brij, who used to help at the farm, and dad returned to Greater Kailash.

Later, dad told us that he had a blackout for a few moments that evening at the house whilst sitting at the dining table. When he came around, he had loose motions. This had never happened before, and it really upset him, and he explained to Krishan that he wanted to return to London immediately. These were the first signs of his illness.

Dad came back to London in July 1993, and it was a good summer. He told us all what had happened in Delhi, with the blackout and loose motions incident. He was also very concerned about his health, was slimmer, and had lost weight. Also, he looked weak. I wanted dad to be checked and ensure he got the best medical assistance.

He was referred to King George Hospital under the NHS, and the test results were taking long. So, I decided to get him checked up by a specialist at The Cromwell Hospital. The results came very quickly, as it was privately funded. It was diagnosed that he had Liver Cancer, which was in its final stage. The specialist advised that we should make him comfortable and take him home. The cancer was harsh, and there was no cure. I think they said he had weeks or a month or so to live. We were to undergo yet another nightmare as we did so in 1981 with the death of our mother.

The news was shocking, and we were not prepared for it. Within a few months of him coming back from India, it happened so fast. His health began to deteriorate very quickly; he lost weight and started to look frail. Everybody was informed, including close relatives and friends. Nothing could save him now. Dad was going to pass away.

As dad was deeply religious and prayed twice daily without fail, we set up a makeshift temple in his bedroom. We did our best to make him comfortable. However, he was aware that he was not well. Friends and relatives were coming to see him. We also made indirect attempts to ask him if he wanted anything or had any unfulfilled wishes. However, we could not bring ourselves to tell him that he had only days to live. It would have broken him. As I have grown up over the years, my view is different and that the patient should be told, so that any final unfulfilled requests may be met.

On 27th August 1993, dad's 73rd birthday and sadly his last was celebrated at Norfolk Road. All our relatives had gathered to wish him. He appeared to be happy but was very frail. He blew out the candles on his birthday cake. All the youngsters in the family made a special effort; they hugged him and sang 'Happy Birthday'. Brave as he was, he tried his best to laugh and appear as if all was well in his last few days.

We never told him that he had cancer, but I believe he knew because he used to bring up the subject of mum's incident and how she was taken from us. He spoke about the pain and heartache.

We took him to King George Hospital on 1st September 1993 because his health was deteriorating at home, and he was losing blood.

Then came 2nd September 1993. I had told myself that I would spend considerable time with him on this day, so I finished my work at the office and came to Norfolk Road. Many people had gathered there, and all of them were talking about dad and his health. They wanted to visit him at the hospital, but too many people were there already, which upset the hospital staff. My brother Ashok's wife Renu mentioned to me that dad was constantly asking for me and that I should go to see him at the hospital. I immediately left for the hospital around 6 pm that evening to spend some quiet time with him. When I got to the hospital ward, it was like a circus! There must have been over 30 visitors there from our side. I decided this was not right and arranged some orderly movement of the visitors. Some people were sent home.

I was able to get a few precious moments with my father by his bedside. I held his hand and assured him that all would be fine. He told me to look after Krishan, my younger brother. His breathing had become difficult by now. He had an oxygen mask over his mouth and quickly lost blood. The nurses tried their best to revive him. We just wanted him to live and survive. The nurses transfused more blood into his system during the last hour or so, but it wasn't bearing positive results. After a while, they stopped and told us to prepare for the worst. I recall even getting angry with the doctors and nurses about why they stopped transfusing blood. They knew his time had come. It was time to let him go.

Around 7:50 pm, on 2nd September 1993, dad breathed his last. I was next to him and held his hand tightly till the very end. Everyone started to cry. He was very well-respected and an elder in the family - a proud, disciplined and simple man full of life. It was the end of an era; now, we had lost both our parents. Once again, I experienced that empty feeling that I had felt when mum passed away in 1981.

A few moments after he passed, the hospital staff gave us his personal belongings. When they removed his two rings, I took one of the gold rings, which he always wore. I said that I wanted to keep it as a reminder. I still wear that ring along with my mother's one on my left hand, both on each finger. My brothers, who were there, were not so pleased about the fact that I had taken the ring. They believed we should share the ring. I simply did not pay any attention. I will wear both these rings till I die.

Raj, my elder brother, took charge of the funeral arrangements, along with Krishan's father-in-law, Bill Bajpai. Dad's funeral was difficult. Many attendees were present at The Manor Park Cremation.

Dad was gone in a matter of months. It just happened so fast; we could not come to terms. Maybe I could ask him when I finally join him in the heavens above.

Life's regret is that we could not share the wealth with our parents. They had seen so many difficult times, worked so hard to make our lives better. Once days became better for the family, they never had any demands. They were just simple, loving and caring parents, who only wanted the best for their children.

Their one desire was to visit the United States of America for holidays, but when plans were underway, our mother sadly fell ill. In the summer of 1980, they managed a memorable visit to Kuala Lumpur and Singapore on Aeroflot. This would be their one and only vacation together. Satish and I had gone to see them off at LHR Terminal 2.

Smt Indra Sharma Bhardwaj. Born 8th March 1930 and passed 4th September 1981 at 5:15 am at Barking Hospital, Upney Lane, Barking, Essex.

Pandit Kul Bhushen Jasuja Bhardwaj. Born 27th August 1920 and passed 2nd September 1993 at 7:50 pm at King George Hospital Goodmayes Road, Ilford Essex. The elders of the Dynasty were gone but will never be forgotten.

Urmil, Mum & Raj

The Six Kumar Brothers

Tony, Mum, Krishan & Suresh

Dad

Dad at Indra Travel

Dad & Suresh

Dad & Pandit Nath Ram Sharma

Chapter 6

Walking in Life with You, Mona!

I first laid eyes on Mona in September 1981. I was 18 and Mona was 17. This eventful scenario came about as we had gone to India with my mother's ashes and to visit our village Kitna in Punjab. While in Punjab, we stayed at the Gautam's house in Model Town, who were the family of Dr Subash Gautam of London, a close family friend in Phagwara. We knew my sister-in-law, Punam Kumar's family well, as there was already a family connection with Mona's family and ours. Punam was married to my older brother Tony on 14th October 1978 in Phagwara Punjab. Furthermore, she was Mona's father, Parshotam's younger sister. So, we were related to the Sharma family in more ways than one. Punam was graceful and full of life and quickly fit into the family. She spent much time in London whilst Tony looked after the Pan Am operations in Frankfurt.

In 1981, I travelled with my mother's ashes to Hardiwar and afterwards travelled to Phagwara. We were staying with our friends, the Gautam's in Model Town. I had heard so much about Punam's family that I was keen to meet them on the visit to Phagwara. I had been unable to attend Tony and Punam's wedding in India in 1978; therefore, I asked Anwar Gautam to take me to their factory on Old Post Office Road and the shop in Banswala Bazaar. They had an ice and soda water factory and made India's best Doodh Soda Milk Almonds Drink. Mr Parshotam Lal Sharma, aka Mangi, Mona's father, was a tall handsome man. He had studied and played football with legendary Indian Film

Star Dharmendra, who was also from Phagwara. They were good friends. He was delighted to see me, and out came the black-label whisky. He was unaware I did not drink whisky; I settled for beer. They had a function to attend that evening, and I was asked to accompany them.

A grey Ambassador car pulled up outside their shop in Bazar Bansawala in Phagwara, and I jumped in the front seat. I saw three girls sitting in the rear seat. I made eye contact with one of the young girls sitting in the corner next to the window. It was Mona that I glanced at and I fell in love with her that evening. When we got to the Rotary function, we were introduced. I was a shy young man from London, and they tried to make fun and laugh at my expense. I was on my best behaviour.

After the function ended, we headed back to the house, through the alleyways and narrow streets, which I was not accustomed to, being from London. It was my first visit to India after Raj's marriage in 1969, and now it was 1981. A lot had changed. Revisiting Punjab as an 18-year-old, I felt that I had grown up and was more aware of my surroundings. I found Punjab and India fascinating and really enjoyed all that it had to offer.

At the house, I met her mother, grandparents, and four siblings. I guess the Sharma family liked me. I like to believe that I left an everlasting impression. But I never forgot the young girl I had met that day in Phagwara.

I was invited to stay that night, an invitation I couldn't refuse. In the morning, I was treated well and served breakfast.

We had set up a Pan Am office in Phagwara. Thereafter, I just needed an excuse to travel to Phagwara every year, only so that I could see and observe that young girl.

I was in love with Mona. I wanted to get to know and study her habits. I wanted to be sure, that she was the right girl for me to marry. She was smart and independent, well-educated and beautiful. I used to think that my children would look good if they took after her. Weren't these selfish thoughts! However, I had made up my mind. Now the master plan had to be executed, to achieve my goal.

On one of my annual visits to Phagwara to meet Mona, we all used to play cards and chat till the wee hours of the morning. I made sure that no one could guess my agenda. I couldn't dare to tell anyone, especially Mona, particularly because I did not know how she would react. If I told her of my feelings, would she feel the same way or simply say no. If she rejected me, that would be the end of that. I had to tread carefully and softly. It was a sensitive matter, which had to be handled with much patience.

Mona's mother's name was Ravi Sharma. Mona has two sisters, the eldest being Meenu and the youngest Anju. Anju is married to Nipan Bhardwaj, from Ealing, West London. Mona has two younger brothers, Bunti and Ashoo, both married and reside with their families in Punjab.

After four years of consecutive visits to Phagwara, an opportunity presented itself in 1984. I had to first convince the family, then the siblings, and finally Mona.

In 1984, Mona's father, Parshotham Lal Sharma, was in London, along with her sister Meenu, dealing with some family matters, and they were staying with us.

One evening in December 1984, as I returned from Empire Travel in London, I was surprised to see a picture of a boy placed on the mantelpiece. He looked Indian. I inquired about the photo, Meenu said, *"It's a boy that has been chosen for Mona, my younger sister."* I was taken aback, as I had set my mind on marrying Mona.

I had very little time to put a plan of action into play. Firstly, I went all out to impress Mona's father. Naturally, I really wanted to assist them with their problems, as they would likely be my in-laws in the future, and I would be doing this for my future wife. My reasons were correct, not just selfish. The family much appreciated my efforts.

January 1985, it was time for Mona's father to head back to India, Meenu stayed behind with our family, where she was well looked after. I planned that we also fly out on Pan Am, on the same flight as Mr Sharma was booked. I asked my father to join us and his brother, Varinder, a jolly good man who could easily interact with the family's men and the younger generation. He was well respected. I asked to come along as a backup plan.

It was all set. We all travelled together in First Class on Pan Am flight 002 to New Delhi. I arranged things in such a manner that Mona's father and my dad sat together, and Uncle Varinder and I sat together in the seats behind. My dad had nine hours to make it happen and work things out with Mr Sharma regarding my marriage to Mona.

But, before all this, I knew I had to have a conversation with my father and explain to him that I was ready for marriage and wanted to marry Mona. He was fond of her. He regularly visited Phagwara en route to our village Kitna and would stop to meet the family in Phagwara.

I sat with him in his bedroom at Norfolk Road and explained my feelings towards Mona. I explained that we needed support in the house to look after us, as Punam could not be away from Tony for extended periods, given that he was running the Frankfurt office and they had young girls. My father agreed. But he wanted to run it through Punam and Tony, as it was her family first. Once we got their blessings and then the plan was set. My father had nine hours to make the case that I would be suitable for Mona.

Pan Am 002 felt like a long flight that day on a cold and wet January morning. I kept trying to listen to their conversation, but there was too much noise coming from the jet engines; I could not do anything about that. Anyway, we arrived in Delhi, and all the signs of the conversation were positive. But nothing was discussed. In a nutshell, Mr Sharma was pleased and said that he would travel that morning to Phagwara and speak with his father,

Shri Nath Ram, take his blessings and make the arrangements to receive us after seven days. I was on cloud nine, and all was going well, as planned. I was counting down the days as a mystical feeling of warmth overtook me.

I did all the shopping in a big rush, the engagement ring, a gold set and a few sarees for Mona. All the jewellery was purchased from Rajiv and Sangeeta Gupta of Shri Ram, Hari Ram of Chandni Chowk in Delhi.

After seven days, we travelled, as agreed to Phagwara by road. The journey took forever, but we were greeted warmly upon our arrival. After nine hours, we reached our destination early in the evening. I was delighted to see the family, especially Mona, but she was unaware of anything at this stage. Her family had not discussed anything regarding my proposal with her. She thought that we were visiting them, as usual. Mona always got on well with my father and Uncle Varinder. They were very fond of her and would regularly say over the years that he would like a bride like her to become a part of our family. That was all about to come true... or was it?

The first day passed, and then the second. We were made to feel special and comfortable. We stayed in the house, however, no one talked about the reason for our visit, i.e., Mona's engagement with me. Had something gone wrong? Had Mr Sharma changed his mind on arrival in Phagwara? More important, had Mona said no. There could be no marriage without the bride. What had happened? Different thoughts were exploding in my mind, and I became very restless.

My father was getting frustrated. Being the elder, he had made his case and was waiting for Mona's father to confirm that they would give me Mona's hand in marriage. Mr Sharma kept quiet, and no one from Mona's family was talking about it. Dad was on the verge of giving up and decided we would leave and head back to New Delhi the following day. He felt disrespected, and rightly so. I could not allow this to happen, so I decided to discuss the matter with Uncle Varinder, who calmed my dad and said let's take it easy. But he was having none of it and was getting upset. He disliked the fact that Mr Sharma was maintaining silence on such an important matter. He wondered what the reason was behind this silence. I sensed that Mona's mother was feeling the cold treatment from my dad as he threw tantrums to let it be known that he was not pleased.

Desperate times require drastic measures. So, that evening, before heading back to New Delhi the following day, empty-handed and without getting engaged to Mona, I did something unheard of and knocked on Mr Sharma's bedroom door around 10:30 pm. I explained what was happening and the sudden morning departure back to New Delhi. I told him that my dad felt that he had been insulted. I explained that our reason for coming to Phagwara was to request my engagement with Mona. He was surprised, as he thought we had changed our minds and were not talking about our engagement. They did not wish to raise it and felt that my dad would get the ball rolling. Mr Sharma assured me that all would be taken care of and that all the arrangements would be made by the morning. I thanked him and returned to put my head down for the night with a sigh of relief. Mr Sharma was a gentle and soft-spoken man who really enjoyed life and would do anything for his family. True to his word, all was moving forward. At sunrise, Mr Sharma had taken the blessing of his father, Shri Nath Ram and spoken to his wife, Ravi and, I guess, to the kids as well. At this stage, Mona was asked by her mother what she thought of me and living in London, and she said no, reasoning that she did not wish to be away from India. Her mother asked if the boy was not right, had any bad habits, or if she disliked me but she denied all and said only living away from her family in the UK was the main reason.

I wanted to make sure that Mona was comfortable with the arrangements, and during that day, I asked if I could speak with Mona in private. Her mother said fine, she wanted us to talk quietly on the veranda, rear garden. Mona brought out a soft drink for me. I remember to date that it was a Limca, a local Lemonade drink.

I was at my best and ready with some well-versed filmi dialogue and asked her to marry me. I said something to the effect that my father wanted her to be my bride, and I wanted her to be my life partner, something similar to the dialogues from the film Aradhana, starring Rajesh Khanna and Sharmila Tagore. She blushed and ran inside. I guess she said, "Yes," as we were to be engaged a few days later. Come to think of it, she never said yes.

After the announcement, calls immediately went out to London to Urmil, Raj's wife; Punam, Tony's wife; Kavita, Raj's eldest daughter and Tina and Reena, Tony's daughters. They were asked to attend, and local relatives were invited, my mother's sister's, Auntie Mohni and Auntie Savitri from Jalandhar, Punjab. Mona's relatives were also invited. A date had been fixed for the engagement ring ceremony, 18th February 1985, at the Phagwara home of the Sharma Family.

On this occasion, my mission had not turned out to be impossible; it was a success. I had pulled it off, and I was to marry Mona. The love of my life, whom I have fallen in love with, when I saw her for the first time in September 1981.

Nonetheless, with my return, a period of writing romantic letters began, and calls were made to each other; the long-distance courtship was in full swing. Telephones in those days were not direct dialling, and calls had to be booked with STD Operators. On occasion, Mona would come to Ludhiana to her aunt's, and we could get some chat time.

It was an outstanding engagement held at Mona's residence, and everyone was pleased, especially my dad and uncle. It was to be a sad parting when we were to head back to New Delhi and then London. We were now engaged, and I felt very sad that I had to leave her behind. It was a very shallow feeling, and I was not too fond of it. With a heavy heart, we departed from Phagwara, and as we drove away, I could see Mona in the rear window, waving at us. Sad… but that's life.

In the 1980s, the UK immigration policy was very long-winded, and a queue system was in place. It could take several months for Mona to get to London. This was not acceptable to me. I wanted to get her by my side quicker.

A very dear friend of mine, Prem Kalra of Rajdoot Hotel, Mathara Road, New Delhi, was well connected in political circles in Delhi. He was close to the President's family, Giani Zail Singh. Living without Mona was difficult, and life was not the same again. I had to get her over to London, so she could be with my family and me.

A plan occurred to me. I announced to the family that immigration laws were changing and that there was a deadline for Mona to come to London, and that was 21st August 1985. I needed someone I could trust to collect Mona from Phagwara, Punjab and put her on a Pan Am flight to London. That was to be my trusted friend Prem Kalra. He was given the task, and he pulled it off with great charm and wit and with soft gloves.

A call rang out from the President's House from New Delhi to Mona's telephone exchange in Phagwara that there was an urgent call from the President's House. It was Prem who was making the call. There was a buzz in Phagwara like never before. Why was the President calling the Sharma family? Telephone exchange became very hot with rumours in Phagwara that evening in August 1985.

Prem was given clear guidelines to go personally to Phagwara and collect Mona and, with kid gloves, bring her to New Delhi and put her on the Pan Am flight to London. He was a bold-looking guy and had a heavy build. He looked like Mr T from the A-Team. However, he was very gentle and very loving.

When he reached Mona's family home in Phagwara after a nine-hour drive and knocked on the door, nobody answered.

They thought some hood had come to the door. Prem explained that I had sent him.

Mona was not to be sent alone with Prem. This was the family's decision, and Ravi, Mona's mother and her brother Ashoo came along to New Delhi. Those were a rushing few days and she hardly had any time for shopping and gathering her stuff. But she was now at Prem's Rajdoot Hotel and ready to depart for London. Mona was quite unwell during these days, as she had an infection.

Pan Am 001 was coming to London via Frankfurt in those days, and there was a plane change. I decided to travel to Frankfurt to meet Mona and ensure that she had no difficulty with immigration and passport control. My family was not pleased with me going to Frankfurt to meet her.

On arrival in London, a big reception awaited us as we crossed the exit doors at LHR terminal 3 Arrivals. Mona was at last, where she belonged, by my side in London. Thank you to Prem, Indu and the Kalra family for their support during this time. We lost sweet Indu Kalra in later years to cancer. She fought bravely. Her death really shook Prem, and it took some time for him to come to terms with her passing.

As we travelled through London from the airport, I pointed out all the landmarks during the drive home. Then we arrived at Norfolk Road but could not stay in the same house, as we were not officially married in the UK, as per traditional Indian custom. So, it was felt that Mona should stay with Raj's family in South Woodford, Essex until the marriage could occur. There had to be a way around this, I thought to myself. But would it be acceptable to everyone?

Anyway, we got home, and I showed her around the place. She felt the houses in London were like matchboxes, all similar looking.

The Court Registration Marriage was fixed for 24th August 1985, and it was agreed that we could live together at Norfolk

Road after that, but in separate rooms. That would have to do for now.

The Court wedding was a grand affair and an opportunity for all the family to get together and have some long-awaited fun. It had been a while since there was a family wedding. We were engaged at Queen Victoria House, Cranbrook Road, in Barkingside.

Our marriage date was fixed for 27 Oct 1985, and the venue was to be Tiffany's, aka the Ilford Palais at Ilford. It was to be a grand venue, over two floors and the grand marriage, which would be talked about for many years thereafter.

Invites were sent out. The wedding cards and flowers for decorations all came from India. The mangos, the sweets; it was wild. Prem and Babu Kalra, Akbar Ahmed, Vasundhara Raje, former CM of Rajasthan, the Khans from LAX, USA, and friends from Germany all came over to attend the marriage ceremony. It was an international affair.

On the day of our marriage, we decorated the venue till 5 pm, before the guests arrived. I had taken too much on and was too involved with the arrangements, with little help. We were to use my brother Satish's gold colour Mercedes as the wedding car. SK BIG was the number plate of the wedding car. The car was decorated with fresh flowers from Delhi. Just before leaving for the hall, the car keys mystically vanished and reappeared after 30 minutes. Everyone was drastically searching for the car keys. You could not make this up as we went along. We made it to the hall in the nick of time.

Mona was wearing a handmade red and gold lehnga wedding dress, and I wore a cream/white Achkan tailor-made in New Delhi. There were around 700 guests invited, and it was a grand Royal Wedding. At the end of the day, we were both so tired. Nonetheless, it had been an eventful day. My dream of marriage to Mona had come true, and it had happened only with God's blessings. I will be forever grateful.

Mona has always stood by me through the good and not so good times. She has been my rock. During her life with me so far, she should never have had to experience those challenges which we faced head-on together. Over the years, her health has suffered. Her family have also been a pillar of support. Her mother and father, the two boys, Bunti and Ashoo, have stood firm and came to stand shoulder to shoulder whenever they were called upon. I am grateful to them all.

It's a wonderful feeling to become a father for the first time and words cannot describe the emotional when you see your child for the first time enter this world. I was elated and wanted to shout from the roof tops, that I was a father. When Megha was delivered at Barking Hospital, soon thereafter the first call I made was to my father to share the good news, that a baby girl was blessed upon us. He was very excited about the news.

Mona and I are blessed with two lovely daughters, Megha and Ektaa. Mona had named Megha, which translates to clouds bearing rain and I named Ektaa meaning unity. Daughters are special and no different to boys. Megha was born in 1988 and Ektaa in 1991, both at Barking Hospital. Megha and Ektaa both commenced schooling at Montessori Day Nursery in Cranbrook Road, Ilford and then at Glenarm College in Coventry Road, Ilford. Thereafter, Megha went on to Bancroft's in Woodford and Ektaa to Oaks Park School. Megha concluded her studies at LSE and Ektaa at Queen Marys. After that, they embarked on full-time employment.

They both are independent and hard-working girls. Both Mona and I are incredibly proud of them. We are very grateful for their unconditional love, care and support always.

They both were born whilst we were still living at the family house. With the growing family, we needed more space. After much soul searching and with sadness and a heavy heart, Mona, Megha, Ektaa and I, left the family home at Norfolk Road in February 1992. It was cold and snowy. I had done up the flats above the office at 791 Romford Road, and it was comfortable enough for the four of us to stay.

We shifted some of our belongings to the flat and settled down. Since we were now living on the main street, it was quite different, and the noise was apparent. We had never lived in a flat. We had a backyard, and Mona and I re-turfed the lawn on a Sunday afternoon in spring. The delivery man had left the lawn layers on the sidewalk outside the office, and we had to hand-carry them through the office and into the back garden. And boy they were heavy loads! Carefully we laid the lawn and cut it into pieces where required. It took us all afternoon, which was another new experience. Working hands in action, Mona and I made a great team.

After residing a few years in the flat, we bought our home, which was closer to the family house. Both girls would have friends and cousins over for their birthday parties, Easter egg hunt parties and Christmas Parties. We were always around them whilst they were growing up.

We always wanted our children to be confident, motivated and self-reliant, they were enrolled in various extracurricular activities from a young age. They loved music and dance and were enrolled to Honey Kalarias Dance Academy in Seven Kings. They performed at Wembley Arena, in the Little Stars show organised by famous Bollywood Music Director, Kalyanji Anandji, who worked closely with Kishore Kumar and produced many classic songs. This gave them much confidence. They have performed for charity, community shows, and even The Conservative Party fundraising. Over the years, various Redbridge Mayors Charity and The Extravagant New Year's Day Parade in Hyde Park, Piccadilly and Westminster.

As any father I wanted the best for my children. Education was always a priority, but so was the real world and for them to have different experiences of life and what it had to offer. Many a time we would pack a basket and drive for an adventure.

I wanted both Megha and Ektaa to be full of confidence and be able to debate and discuss issues, that they may be confronted with in life. That's why I had them participate in the shows and events, to interact with an audience. Dance and the arts were always an important ingredient and gave them much joy and acceleration.

It was important for our children to be aware of our roots from India, as well as the western culture and festivals here in the UK. One of many highlights each year with Megha and Ektaa was the Easter Egg hunt. On each Easter Sunday, before the kids were up, I would place easter eggs in small see through containers around the garden, hidden out of sight and for them to find. Sometimes their friends were invited to join. I recall Ektaa was always looking forward to finding the Easter eggs and eating them.

Whilst Megha and Ektaa were growing up, we would make it a point to travel to India at least once a year and for them to understand and stay connected to our culture and for them never to lose sight of their heritage. At home we would converse in English and Hindi Punjabi. They were connected to Bollywood films, through my love of Rajesh Khanna and Kishore Kumar. These films were helpful for them to understand the language and see how people interacted with each other. At a young age they were enrolled at Honeys Dance Academy at Seven Kings to learn Bollywood dance and they participated in many shows, that Honey Kalaria would put together for her students. Honey has remained a close friend over the years and has given a vital service to the community. She has done a lot of work with the young. We have done many shows and events together in support of charities and promoting Indian values and culture. She is also a fellow Aquarian, so that explains her drive and determination.

When the Home Alone movies came out, Megha was keen to have a talk boy hand recorder, The original Talk boy was designed as a prop to be used by Macaulay Calkin's character,

Kevin McCallister, in the 1992 film Home Alone 2: Lost in New York. It was her prized possession and she had many good times out and about making recordings.

Megha played the Piano well and had tuition classes. She achieved grade 8 and was able to teach. Megha followed her father's entrepreneurial skills, and one summer holiday, she placed advertising cards in local shop windows and offered piano lessons at £10 per half an hour. She was inundated and even taught her nephew Aaryan. Both girls were encouraged to take school trips and outings. Growing up years were fun; we took regular trips within the UK and holidays abroad. We have remained very close, and the four of us are the four pillars of The Family Foundation. There was a time when Megha was at LSE, and we agreed reluctantly for her to live in halls for the first year. It was a sad and teary-eyed day when we moved her into her halls. It was the first time we were to stay apart. It was an unreal feeling and on a rare occasion, I became emotional.

They both would keep scrapbooks and write notes to members of the family, expressing their thoughts. Once Ektaa, after getting told off by me, wrote a note to my father, who had passed away by this time, advising him that his son, me, was telling her off and that her granddad should tell his son off. But despite that, she still loved her dad very much. I still cherish this note.

Whilst Ektaa was at Queen Mary's University halls staying away from home. At times we would visit her unannounced and surprise her with her favourite food and sweets.

In 1999, one Sunday afternoon, whilst Megha and Ektaa were visiting their cousins on Norfolk Road, Ektaa met with a serious road accident. The young girls, Esha, Megha and Ektaa were playing in the front garden and on hearing the music of the ice cream van, Ektaa ran out into the road, as it had parked across the road and would have headed down towards Meads Lane. Sadly, she did not stop and look left, right and left again as per the green cross code, but ran into the road, towards the ice cream van. A BMW travelling very fast hit her on the leg and luckily, she fell backwards and was in severe pain from the impact. Everyone came rushing out into the road, Punam, my sister-in-law, Megha, Esha and the surrounding neighbours. They tried to comfort her on the road, as Mona and I got a frantic call on the mobile from Megha. She was crying, as I answered the phone and instantly, I knew that something terrible had happened. I told her to be calm and slowly explain what had just happened. I told her to be with Ektaa and call the ambulance, which they had already done. A neighbour from across the road had already put Ektaa into a recovery position as she knew First Aid. Mona and I were in the car on Eastern Avenue, with Tina, my niece, headed very fast towards Norfolk Road. My immediate reaction was to turn the front lights on full, even though it was light and around 4 pm and I sounded the horn, for other cars to move out of my way. This was an emergency, and my vehicle had become so. I jumped the red lights at speed at the junction of Aldborough South and North, headed towards Norfolk Road. I turned left onto Cameron Road and first left into Norfolk Road. As we turned the car, we saw Ektaa lying on the floor, with Punam comforting her and a blanket placed on her to keep her warm, as the ambulance had not arrived by the time we got there. I parked the car in the middle of the road, so that other cars would not pass, as it could be dangerous for Ektaa and others, looking after her. I rushed over to her and sat down behind her head and put her head in my lap and talked to her. She was in a lot of pain and in semi-shock. I shouted to ask, where the ambulance was? It was on the way, someone shouted back. It took forever. By now there must have been 30 or so people looking after Ektaa and some who had come out of their homes to offer comfort, we had lived at Norfolk Road since 1976, and were well known. The driver of the BMW a young guy, who had pulled over after the impact, was also in a state of shock and kept saying she ran into the road and was apologetic. I told Ektaa not to worry, she will be fine and held her hand tightly. After 20 minutes or so the ambulance arrived and took charge. They initially assessed Ektaa and confirmed that it was a fracture and off she went to King George Hospital, I jumped into the ambulance with her. Whilst others followed. King George Hospital took good care of Ektaa and after several days she was discharged with her leg in a plaster and plenty of painkillers. Ektaa was in a better state of mind, as the initial shock had passed and to keep her in good spirits, we were all trying to make her laugh and tell jokes. She was given a pair of crutches and explained how to use them. How can I explain how I felt, as a father, seeing one's daughter lying in the road and thinking the worse? As if the earth was taken from under my feet. In the coming months, Ektaa recovered well and still carries a scar to remind her of the accident.

Another funny incident comes to mind. Megha started work once she completed her graduation. Whilst on a work-related trip to Dubai, she was told firmly to call us or text at least once a day to let us know that she was fine. Except once, when it was late in the evening in the UK and there was no message from Megha. She was at a work event earlier and then went to a club with some work colleagues and friends. Unaware, I was worried for her safety. I called the hotel in Dubai and requested them to ask Megha to contact me immediately as soon as she returns. I made several calls to reach her, but there was no reply, as her mobile phone battery was dead.

As soon as Megha reached the hotel room, she saw a man stationed outside her room on a chair. Immediately after seeing Megha, the man got up from his seat and informed Megha about the messages from her dad and how concerned he was. He followed Megha into her room and advised her to call her dad right away as being a father himself, he could relate to my feelings. Bless him! The hotel staff did not leave Megha until she had made the call. Megha was amused and started laughing and called me.

I am sure many parents would have experienced this in their lifetime. It's funny, but Mona, Megha, Ektaa and I really enjoy each other's company, we holiday together and do things as a family unit. Celebration of each other's birthdays are a treat and different themes are sought and actioned, mainly as a surprise. Our relationship has become more like friends, and we share many things as a family. The younger generations of the family get on well with each other, have similar ages and have strong bonds with each other. They have carried the family traditions forward of keeping close and looking out for each other. They have surrounded themselves with good caring friends who meet regularly and even holiday together. In relationships, it's all about caring and looking out for one another. We enjoy their friends coming over and spending time at the family home. They enjoy sleepovers, watching movies, hanging out, enjoying life, and having fun.

In later years, when it was time for Megha and Ektaa to settle down, they found amazing partners in Rajiv Mehta and Ishraj Aytan and the bonding of families.

Naresh Uncle, Swarna Auntie, Dad, Mona, Suresh, Prakash Auntie, Varinder Uncle
Aug 1985

Suresh & Mona's Wedding Oct 1985 Ilford Palais

Tony, Krishan, Satish, Mona, Suresh, Ashok, Bob, Raj, Aug 1985

Suresh, Mona & Newly born Megha Feb 1988

Megha & Suresh 1989

Megha & Suresh 1989

Suresh, Megha & Newly born Ektaa June 1991

Ektaa, Suresh & Megha 1992 @ Margate Beach

Megha, Suresh & Ektaa 1994

Mona, Ektaa, Suresh & Megha @ Glenarm School Sports Day

Megha & Suresh

Ektaa, Suresh & Megha

Suresh & Mona

Ektaa, Suresh, Megha & Mona Holiday at Maldives

Ektaa, Suresh, Megha 25ᵗʰ Wedding Anniversary

Parshotham Lal & Ravi Sharma - Mona's Parents

Ravi Sharma & Mona

Suresh, Ektaa, Megha & Mona

Parshotham Lal Sharma

Suresh @ India Cricket Match

Chapter 7

Rising Star Politics

Historically, my family voted for the Labour Party and in my younger days, I may have as well on instructions from my parents. There was this myth that the Labour Party were for the working class, hence many Asians would vote for them, without even understanding their manifest and policies. As I grew older, I started to question this myth and began to ask questions and investigate their policies. My values were more in tune with the Conservative Party.

From an early age, during my growing up years, I always was interested in politics. The years 1996/1997 saw me eager to join politics, so why not start at the top? I wrote to the then Prime Minister, John Major. My values in life were closely aligned with the Conservative Party and allowed people to define their destiny. Traditionalist conservatism is a political philosophy emphasising the need for the principles of natural law and transcendent moral order, tradition, hierarchy, and organic unity. However, my family voted for Labour. Margaret Thatcher inspired me with her strong leadership and for improving the lives of the ordinary British people by making the country a better place.

The PM's office asked me to contact Sir Graham Bright, who introduced me to Sir Neil Thorne, my local MP for Ilford South. The Tories were in bad shape, and it was clear that Tony Blair would win the next general election in 1997. Since we lived in Ilford South, it was the constituency that I was hooked up with. Having been referred to Sir Graham Bright, I met him at Central Office at Smith Square, in a small office. I also met Sir Neil

Thorne OBE, the former Member of Parliament for Ilford South from 1987 to 1992, and the year in which he lost the seat by 402 votes to Labours Mike Gapes. They required assistance for the election, so the two suggested that I could help garner the Asian vote, which would be crucial for the Tories.

On another occasion, I met Sir Neil Thorne and Elizabeth Hunt at their home on Holcombe Road in Ilford. They gave me an overview of local affairs and the political landscape in Ilford. Ilford South Conservatives was a dying association like so many across the country. They had limited funds, and the good days of the Blues were dwindling fast.

Ilford South, the Parliamentary constituency has nine wards, Mayfield, Seven Kings, Cranbrook, Clementswood, Goodmayes, Loxford, Newbury Park, Valentines, and Chadwell Heath. Each ward has a Deputy Chair and a Chairman. Some of the wards were ineffective, and their structure needed to be revised. It could be seen that the Tory membership was ageing, and members were leaving at a fast rate. The change was in the air as the country was being swept with The Tony Blair fever.

In 1997, prior to the general elections, I was invited to a ceremony to honour a fallen policeman, PC Walters, in Empress Avenue Ilford. Tony Blair was the chief guest. I got the opportunity to meet him briefly, and we exchanged pleasantries. It was said that Tony Blair was a Labourite in Tory clothing. He spoke the language of Labour and added a Tory policy to his statements. He bore the likeness of a true salesman speaking a modernising language, which appealed to the masses looking for a change. The public had seemingly had enough of the Tories and did not want them in office again. Tony Blair was full of charm and glamour and soon had people eating out of his palms.

In 1997, a fundraising event was organised by Ilford South Conservative Association at the Penthouse Suite on High Road. I was invited to meet some locals, and I observed that young people were scarce while senior citizens could be seen in abundance.

The number of attendees neared a hundred, and on every table, a brown envelope was placed to collect donations. I recall that I donated £20.

I shared a table with Surendra and Usha Patel of Gordon Road, Ilford. Over the coming years, we became friends. However, the fact is that the experience was not what I had expected. Nonetheless, I always loved a challenge. Time was short, and the general election was fast approaching.

Earlier, Sir Neil had Mick White as a close aide and a loyal Conservative. Mick White later became Leader of the Havering Council. Since I was working closely with Mick White on many issues for the election, it was a given that we would get to know each other better. Mick White observed me and the work I did for a few weeks and saw how I was making circumstances change for the better. I involved more people from various backgrounds and brought in young blood to fight for the cause.

He once said, *"If only you had been sent a year ago, we would have had a fighting chance in Ilford South."* However, the way I looked at it, all was not lost. We were going to put up a good fight and give Labour a run.

Elizabeth Hunt was Chair of Ilford South Conservatives and I toiled for many long hours to get the wards in shape. She was a very supportive person and guided me throughout the process. However, we had very few people on the ground. Despite the height of the power struggle between the different communities, we managed to even things out and take everyone forward together. I managed to gain quite a following along the way. After all, I was a young businessman, throwing my weight around.

I meant business and went about bringing immediate change across the Conservative Party in Redbridge and communicated the same to the masses, thus activating and channelling critical people from some communities. These people took our message to the broader community. It was apparent that by this time, we were in better shape.

My background was in the world of business. Watching Labour's extensive PR and media approach, I understood the relevance of PR activities and media presence in the modern face of politics. And that brought forward the need to raise more funds locally.

In 1997, just before the general elections, John Major, a friend of Sir Neil Thorne OBE, visited us. When John Major was contesting in the elections as Leader of the Conservative Party, Sir Neil had made his Westminster home at Cowley Street, available for Campaign HQ. He had promised a visit to support Sir Neil Thorne in his campaign.

It was a dark, wet, and gloomy afternoon when Sir John Major, the Prime Minister of Great Britain, came to Ilford Town Centre on the Tory Bus. The people welcomed him amidst waving placards and plenty of cheers, as though he was a star. The sight was one to feast your eyes on. He shook hands with the people and greeted the crowds. Then, in the walking promenade, he flashed past his favourite M&S store on Ilford High Road. There was high security at the event, and the visit was kept very quiet till the last moment. After an hour or so, he was back on the campaign bus and on to the next stop for yet another campaign tour, which was the political highlight.

Given that Ilford South was considered a marginal seat, which had lost by only 402 votes in 1992, many VIP visits were planned to support Sir Neil, and he had won much respect and goodwill from within the Tory Party. So, we had visits from Michael Heseltine, Ann Widdecombe, and many more. Thus, I found myself moving with influential people, and the giants of the political world were now approachable.

The Ilford South team looked grave, and I feel they knew within themselves that they would get a bashing at the polls. Meanwhile, Sir Neil and Elizabeth kept the feel-good factor going and carried themselves with confidence and bravely now, the electorate at the national level had lost its confidence in the

Conservatives; there were many divisions within the Party, and allegations of sleaze did not go down well. However, the country had other plans, and in a tidal wave, many seats were lost to Labour. There was no stopping the Tony Blair feel-good factor.

The country seemed to have decided to eliminate the Tories and hand power to Tony Blair and New Labour. Something to ponder over was that the New Labour's policies were, in fact, Tory policies and ideas that had been cleverly disguised as New Labour. The spin and PR machine was in overdrive, and there was no way to stop Blair.

It so happened that the Conservatives were out. Sir John Major was a good and honest man, but the party was disunited and were fighting each other openly. Thus, it was a free fall for all.

Once the general election of 1997 was over, it was time to focus our attention on the 1998 local elections in Redbridge. We searched for good and diverse candidates for the polls and placed them in the wards around the constituency.

Sir Neil Thorne, OBE, a successful businessman in his own right, decided that he would not stand as a Parliamentary Candidate in Ilford South for the party again and took up an advisory role in the Conservative Party, thus spending more time in Westminster. That's when I decided that I wished to have a crack at the Ilford South nomination as a Member of Parliament.

There was much to be done. *Was Ilford South ready for an Asian candidate? Would I be able to gain enough support? Would I upset the traditional indigenous community and most of the Tory membership?* I needed to find answers to these questions. So, I tried to get a feel of public opinion and took a gentle approach. Ilford South seemed to need a breath of fresh air, and I was about to offer them just that.

I believe that it was only correct that I should have discussed my ambitions and thoughts with Sir Neil and Elizabeth. I felt comfortable asking them for advice and thought they would guide me in making a critical decision, i.e., whether I should contest for the seat or wait for the right time. It was inevitable that I would have to fight against the winds of change.

After my meeting, it was evident that the advice was to wait, get some more experience, and sit out the New Labour feel-good factor. The big question was: Was Ilford South ready for an Asian candidate? I took counsel from family, close friends, and business colleagues in and around Redbridge.

Mona believed politics was dirty and would be a thankless task. She was very against my entry into the world of politics. She also felt that I should wait a few years to join active politics. But, knowing how I felt, this was an opportunity not to be missed and she reluctantly supported my cause and stood firm by my side. On the other hand, community leaders felt this was the right time. The business community thought that a voice was needed in support of democracy. In Ilford South, most Tory members were against me contesting in the Redbridge elections. The point to note was that I had developed good ties with some members and was not considered an outsider. The benefit I had was that I was a doer, not just one who stood by and watched others do the graft. I led from the front, and that was what garnered more supporters. But, to win the nomination, I needed some hard-core support.

Our agent in Ilford South, Alan Doran, was based at our party office at Sevenways House Gants Hill. He was a paid agent, and we ensured that he was paid from our fundraising and hard work. He used to update Conservative Central Office about our activities, including the significant increase in diverse Asian membership, which had just soared. There were no financial constraints in Ilford South anymore since much money had been raised through membership, social events, and donations from local businessmen. Things were going well for Ilford South; all that was needed was my one candidate seat approval from The Conservatives Candidates Department.

If I were to contest as a candidate, I only wished to represent Ilford South, my hometown, and where I grew up. I was born in Ilford and lived in Newbury Park. I had lived here all my life, and my roots were firmly in Ilford. I was a local candidate, which allowed me to get one-seat approval. I was asked to meet Lord Feldman, a conservative old-school man looking after candidates' selection at Conservative Central Office. It was a delight to meet him and get the one-seat approval. I was finally on my way, although I felt my approval might be blocked for some odd reason.

Our activities in Ilford South did not go unnoticed by Central Office – Tory HQ as they had heard that good things were happening in our region.

We were raising vital funds for the campaign and increased our profile in the media. I had secured support from the local press. Chris Carter and Claire Borley of the Ilford Recorder, Anthony from The Redbridge Post, Sid Walker from The Yellow Advertiser, and The Guardian Gazette from Woodford were now all supportive. They covered many of our campaigns and activities. It was not easy to acquire widespread coverage in the area without the cooperation of the press, so this was a positive development for our cause.

I knew that it was critical for the public to know my stance on specific issues and that the best way to convey my feelings was to write letters; therefore, I sent many letters each week to these papers. Thankfully, my efforts paid off, and several letters were printed, giving me widespread exposure in the local press.

I would read local and national papers cover to cover, hand-picking stories from which I could take ideas and have them dropped in the letterboxes of the papers every late Sunday evening. Running around and dropping stuff was graciously managed by my wife, Mona and even young Megha and Ektaa. They made vital contributions to the campaign. It was a difficult period, and there was no regard for one's health or personal life. Many sacrifices were made during these political years. I would for sure handle this period differently and with more experience gained. However, the nomination for Ilford South was all that mattered at the time, and we were well on our way.

In 1997 till 2000, I was selected to be a member of The Cultural Unit which was established by the then Leader of The Conservative Party, William Haque MP. This was run from Conservative Central Office and based at Smith Square, London. There were around 20 of us and representing different backgrounds and cultures. We would advise from time to time and look at new ideas to make the Party more inclusive and reaching out to the various communities around the UK.

In 2000, I had the privilege of meeting my Political icon, the Great Margaret Thatcher, Prime Minister of Great Britain, and Leader of The Conservative Party. It was a dream come true for me and my friends from Ilford South. She was humble and we had a chat about the great Conservative victories. She was very supportive and agreed to visit Redbridge and support our activity.

Without having a political Godfather or any experience of politics, in 2000, I was selected as the Conservative Prospective Parliamentary Candidate for Ilford South at a large meeting held at the Lambourne Rooms at Ilford Town Centre. I had asked all the members to come early. The 200 or so seats that were laid out were taken up very quickly. Across the room, you could see a swarm of diverse people. Even the members who had never shown up or attended any meetings were in attendance. Mothers came to the meeting with little children in prams, demonstrating how vital the gathering was, their desire to be a part of the way forward, and, more importantly, to show their support for me. It was incredible, and I will be eternally thankful to all those who supported me. My success was not mine alone, there were so many people behind me in one way or another.

There was a big celebration afterwards at Paul Waraich's Carlton House till the early morning. These were good times, but little did I know at that time that heartache lay ahead. I was caught up in the Political enigma, and all seemed well, but not for long.

With well-wishers by my side, the vultures were also gathering pace, and the whispering campaign had begun. But we stood firm and took them head-on; we weren't going down without a fight.

I began to assemble my inner campaign team, which would serve as a solid foundation of devoted friends and supporters. I didn't trust everyone, which was understandable, and I didn't want the opponents to know our strategy.

Key members of the internal team were Glen and Beatrice Corfield, Jim Howes, Maureen Ashley, Arthur Leggett, Paul Waraich, Jay Patel, Ivy Smith, Surendra Patel, Satish Gautam, Mr K B Joshi, Mark Aron, an old friend from South Park School, Alan Kemp, Habib Rehman, Khalid Hussian of K1 Tyres Ilford Lane, Mary Daly, Mo Sheikh, Darshan Sharma, Mahboob Choudhry, Denis Aylen, Moira and John Quinn, David, Dr Harjit Sura, Darshan Sunger, Saroop Singh Kalsi, Sudharshan Bharjee, Harbans Singh Kallah, Baldev Bassan, David and Taniya Soloman, to name a few. By now, Sir Neil and Elizabeth had decided to take a back seat but were always there to provide us with valuable advice and guidance.

I realised that politics would never be easy, especially for someone with a business and ethnic background, but that was the way it was, and we had to do our best. I visited numerous folks and went out to all the communities in Ilford South. In my mind, I never held discrimination against anyone and treated everyone fairly and equally. We kept a stall in the Ilford Town Centre, prompting Conservative values. One Saturday afternoon, we noticed a guy photographing us all from a distance, and we discovered that he was a reporter planning to publish a story.

The PR media machine was in overdrive. Labour in Ilford South was worried, they had never seen so much coverage for a Tory candidate before. We were everywhere and were saying and doing the right things. My business dealings and history were scrutinised from all angles. My opponent, Labour Party candidate Mike Gapes, was campaigning with teams of ones and twos, but we were out in groups of threes and fours and in different areas simultaneously. Our campaigns were going well. However, I was worried about the credibility of the information gathered by helpers from the electorate. Each evening, the canvass card figures appeared to be optimistic. Yet, I couldn't help but wonder if our inexperienced campaign team's enthusiasm marked the canvas cards with a positive C for Conservative. To enlist the support of the minority communities, advertisements were placed in various newspapers and in various languages.

We maintained high-profile visits to Ilford South with Theresa May, Steve Norris, Jeffrey Archer, Patti Boulaye, Theresa Villiers, Lord Tebbit, and the former Prime Minister, Sir John Major. These visits helped us raise much-needed funds to keep the Association going.

Ilford South shared its offices with Ilford North and Leyton & Wanstead at Sevenways House in Gants Hill, and each paid a share towards the running expenses, making it easier for us to keep our heads down. Of course, we never had much privacy and were looked upon with suspicion. But, as a fact of the matter, we brought in the funds and had the highest profile in the Association.

Another setback was when Dr Liam Fox, the Shadow Health Secretary, agreed to visit Ilford South to meet doctors and medical professionals to discuss the status of King George Hospital. All the preparations had been done, and an event was set to take place at Prabha Suites in Ilford. However, Labour floated rumours that KGH was to be closed. The false stories made Dr Fox pull out at the last minute, citing that an important matter had come up that required his attention. However, the fact is that he could not face the medical personnel. This event was a significant setback, and I'm convinced it cost us vital support in the months ahead and throughout the election. The doctors and nurses were furious and demanded that he meet with them and offer an explanation, but Liam Fox was nowhere to be seen.

Finally, Steve Norris MP, for whom I had worked on his Mayoral Campaign team, stepped in at the last minute and saved the day from total disaster. Steve was a likeable chap with good debating skills and managed to calm the medical people down with his peaceful and soft approach. The day was saved, and we battled on.

In 1999/2000, I had the privilege of working with Lord Archer. He was a breath of fresh air and would have won the election for Mayor of London if he had not decided to resign as the candidate. He had the best people around him and plenty of funds for the campaign. He had an internal team of 15-20 people from diverse backgrounds and ages. There was much experience among them, and they all were loyal to Lord Archer.

The Jeffrey Archer team was having trouble landing a meeting with the High Priest Pramukh Swami Maharaj, at The Neasden Temple in Neasden. MP Nadhim Zahawi approached me in future years to be a Minister in the Conservative Government and Party Chairman. I knew certain people on the Board of the temple and, through my contacts, was able to speak with Suresh Patel, who ran a Post Office in Manor Park. He talked to some trustees, and it was arranged for Lord Archer to visit the temple and have blessings from the Guru. This must have been Thursday, and the visit was arranged for Sunday afternoon.

The Archer team was impressed and could not believe they had gotten an audience. I wanted to be a part of this and decided that we should all meet outside the Neasden Temple on Sunday afternoon. Thankfully Nadhim had already briefed him about my involvement in securing the visit and ensured to give the due credit. In politics, too often, the one who makes all the arrangements never gets the credit. But that was not the case here.

We were all given a grand tour of the facilities, and towards the end of the visit, an audience with Swami Pramukh Ji. He welcomed us, and we had tea and chatted. He presented Lord Archer with a large photo of the main temple in India, the Akshardham Swaminarayan Temple. We were given gifts of flowers, books, and Prasad sweets as we departed.

At the temple, I took photos that I later utilised in my social media profile. Working with the Lord Archer team was fantastic and would open many avenues in the future. They were a gifted group of individuals indeed, and many now have top jobs in the Conservative Government.

Lord Archer thanked both Mona and me. I also got him to sign an autograph because Mona was a big fan of his writing. He was very grateful, and we departed ways. He was impressed with my arrangements and wanted me involved in the campaign, looking after ethnic communities. Soon, I was recruited to be among them.

Teji Mudhar of Sterling Media, an established PR & Media company in London, was a close friend. Her father was a client of mine at Indra Travel in the early 80s before he passed away. He had put me in touch with Teji, So, I asked Teji to support the Lord Archer campaign, and she invited him to several high-profile events where we would take Lord Archer and get him to meet various groups and different communities. It worked well, and we came away with much-secured support for Lord Archers' campaign. Lord Archer was extremely punctual and organised.

We were making a significant impact on the ethnic voters. I learnt from Lord Archer the art of making effective speeches. It is incredible how he builds himself up before a big speaking event and then goes on and performs like an A-list actor. He had a structure to his performance. He was one of a kind and damn good at what he said and how he said it. His speeches never failed to pull the crowd in. He was a stage performer who gave an Oscar-worthy performance each time.

At one event the crowds went wild when he arrived; everyone was in place and seated by now, waiting for the Chief Guest, Lord Archer. He gave an excellent speech and converted all votes in his favour. The waiting crowd of 5000 were not disappointed with Lord Archers' sterling performance. He was converting support all day and making the vote bank grow daily. By now, he was a clear front-runner against Ken Livingstone. But it was all about to come to an abrupt and sad end for Lord Archer.

There were whispers that things were not going well in the Lord Archer camp, and on Saturday, before the News of the World piece on Lord Archer and the Perjury Claims was to be published, I received a call from Lord Archer's secretary. She said, *"The News of the World would publish claims on Sunday. Lord Archer would resign from the campaign, and would like to talk with you and explain himself."*

Lord Archer was on the phone, apologising and quickly explaining what was about to happen and expressing his regret for the excellent bunch of individuals around him, referring to the Archer campaign team. Finally, he said goodbye and thanked me for my help and efforts. He made it apparent that he had no idea what the future had in store for him. Who knew that I would encounter a similar situation in the coming years?

I felt gutted, as we were all so consumed in the Mayoral Campaign to get Lord Archer elected, but now, there was a big void after he stepped down. The hopes of a possible position in the Mayoral team at City Hall were dashed. No one from within the Tory Party came close to a Jeffrey Archer style campaign.

Within days, it was decided that Steve Norris would run for the Tories as the new Mayoral Candidate instead of Lord Archer. The Archer team were summoned to meet Steve and his advisers at Steve's offices in London. But the Archer team was disheartened, and some went away to do other things while the rest supported Steve. I supported Steve and worked well with him in the coming months, but life was never the same as it was with Lord Archer.

Steve Norris put up a brave challenge but entered the race late, and Lord Archer was a difficult act to live up to. However, Steve worked hard and had a respectful share of the votes.

Ken Livingston went on to become the Mayor of London. Steve did not have much chance, as he had come into the race late. Furthermore, after Lord Archers' departure, Steve did not have support from the broader communities. Steve was a great campaigner but was not given credit for his politics.

After the poor results in the General Election of 2001 in Ilford South, where we lost to Mike Gapes of the Labour Party, I still wanted to be a Member of Parliament. I decided that this time, I would work my way up from within the system and decided to put my name forward for the 27th July 2003 Valentines by-election, being held due to the death of a local councillor, Gary Scottow, in Valentines Ward in Ilford South. The Labour majority in this seat was 500 or so. My Labour opponent was a seasoned campaigner Lesley Hilton, who had been an active local voice for the Labour Party. I had minimal local council experience and decided to build up the local ward activity and create a profile.

It became apparent that the Labour party firmly held this seat for several years, and there was little chance for the Tories to sweep it from beneath them and become victors. The campaign became hotly contested, and Labour brought out all their heavy guns, including MP Mike Gapes, Elaine Norman, and Labour Leaders of Redbridge Council, among other established and well-experienced councillors. The Tories felt it was a waste of time and that there was no chance in hell to win the seat.

With the exposure I got from the general election, I became popular with the Asian vote. However, there was a hindrance. People would sometimes promise their vote but would be too busy or not bother to vote on Election Day. The Conservative Party had to secure as many votes as possible, and the only way to achieve this was to advise and encourage the public to send their votes in by proxy or postal votes. By the end of the by-election, the Conservative Party had collected 402 postal and proxy votes. A record in Redbridge and local elections.

Meanwhile, I had gotten to know Steve Norris well, and he visited during the by-election and helped raise the profile of our campaign. We campaigned with Steve in Ilford Town Centre and visited the Balfour Road Mosque. He was well-received by the local community. On the other hand, Councillor Keith Prince and Councillor Aron Powell worked tirelessly during the campaign, along with our team of volunteers.

We had various campaign offices set up within the Valentines Ward, and it helped to move people around. It was a slick election campaign, and we had requested all our voters to vote early, so we don't have to waste time chasing them during the day.

Polls opened at 7:00 am and closed at 10:00 pm, it was a long and arduous campaign. I can proudly declare that we fought till the last minute and rushed voters into the polling stations. We understood that every vote would be needed, and by now, it was clear that the race would be neck to neck. The Labour Party were out in force, bringing in aid from other areas. They could see this seat going to The Tories.

After the polls closed, we headed for the count at Ilford Town Hall and reached there around 10:30 pm when the ballot boxes were beginning to arrive. Many of our supporters were count assistants and assigned to oversee the counting of the votes vigilantly. Other supporters waited outside the Town Hall, anxious to hear the outcome.

The Chief executive of Redbridge Council was Roger Hampson, a charming man. The results after the first count were very close in our favour, and thus, a recount had been requested by Labour. At 12:45 pm Roger Hampson walked onto the Town Hall stage, ready to announce the results. As I glanced at my agent Aron Powell, I could tell he was pleased. The results were read:

"Hilton Lesley, the Labour Party candidate, 1000 votes cast and Kumar, Suresh, The Conservative Party candidate, 1009. I declare Suresh Kumar the newly elected member of Valentines Ward in the London Borough of Redbridge."

I had won, with a tiny margin of 9 votes. I walked towards the mic to give a speech and thanked the many supporters and volunteers. The Labour Party supporters started to boo and could not believe the results. After a tireless effort, it was time to celebrate, and we all headed off to Carlton House at the High Road, Ilford.

This was a significant setback for the Labour Party in Redbridge, and they were unhappy. However, who knew that the effects of their unhappiness would come to bite me in my rear later in my career?

Soon after the results were declared of the Valentine ward by-election and I had been elected as the Councillor, the Labour Party filed a complaint with the Election Office at Queen Victoria House, and the police were called to investigate. The claim was 'Abuse of Proxy Votes.'

The enquiry was held in a somewhat high-handed manner and the police called the proxy voters and the people who cast the votes at all hours of the day to inquire. We were told that there had been some complaints and the police had to investigate. However, we were never shown those complaints for some reason.

Subsequently, I was arrested, questioned by the police, and released on bail. They checked every vote in detail. The investigation lasted for nearly a year, many people were questioned, but nothing came out of it.

In July 2002, my solicitor, Colin Nott of Hallinan, got a call from the police, informing him that the police had dropped the case as there was no evidence found against us.

Mona, Megha, Ektaa, and I were in Punjab, India, at the time with Mona's family, and when the news came in, we were driving back from Shimla. We pulled over and hugged each other for a few moments. Though the case had taken a year to resolve, it was a great relief as a huge burden had been lifted.

I had again seen the ugly side of politics and how false allegations are made to suit one's position. However, in time, I would pay a very high price for my political motivations, a price hefty enough to rock those motivations forever and leave an everlasting impact on my family. It is said, "In Politics, the opponents standing in front of you, whom you can see, may seem to be the enemy, then the so-called friends standing behind you, who are far worse and will stab you in the back at any given chance."

Friends with The Rt Hon Margaret Thatcher PM @ Conservative Party HQ

Trustees of Swaminarayan Temple Neasden with Mona, Suresh & Lord Archer 1999

PM John Major and Suresh @ Room at the Top Ilford 2000

Suresh, PM John Major & Mona @ Room at the Top Ilford 2000

Vaisakhi Mela Suresh and Theresa Villiers MP

1999 Sir Neil Thorne, Elizabeth Hunt & Suresh Award Ceremony

Mona, Lord Norman Tebbit &
Suresh

Suresh and Jeffrey Archer @
Valentinos

2019 PM Boris Johnson & Suresh

Suresh, Loveena, Debashish & Virendra Sharma MP

Chapter 8

The Walk of Fame

Back in the 1970s, our parents used to own a grocery store on Green Lane in Seven Kings that catered to the Asian community in the neighbourhood. Around 1969, when Hindi films became popular, Kundan Singh and Tara Singh, two local businessmen, began to promote them at the Old Odeon Cinema Forest Gate. They would come around and put posters in our front shop windows to attract moviegoers. In exchange, we were given free movie passes. The screenings were mainly held on Sundays with two shows, at 11 am and 2 pm.

The same year, my father took me to see my first Bollywood film, Aradhana, which starred a newcomer named Rajesh Khanna and an established star Sharmila Tagore. From Green Lane, we took bus number 25 to Romford Road Forest Gate. The trip must have taken about 30 minutes. When we arrived for the 2 pm show, the hall was packed, and there was excitement in the air; these are the recollections of when I was a six-year-old - a mere child born in Ilford who was coming to see a Bollywood movie for the first time.

The hall was buzzing, and the audience erupted in applause while whistling could be heard throughout the film. I remember the first few minutes of the movie when a young handsome-looking Rajesh Khanna sat in a jeep with a friend Surjit Kumar and sang a song directed toward the young Sharmila Tagore on the train. The song was *'Mere Sapno Ki Rani,'* which was incredible. The scene for the song was shot separately by both stars. However, in the world of cinematography, the scenes were edited to appear as one.

I'm not sure how much I understood at six years old, but whatever I saw stayed with me forever. This is where my love for Rajesh Khanna and Bollywood began. The film was a smash hit, as it broke all box office records and the first and only superstar of Hindi cinema was born.

Suddenly, I was telling my cousins and brothers about Rajesh Khanna – his acting, mannerisms, and singing voice. I believed that he sang the songs in his movies. It was much later that I found out the reality. To my surprise, the dazzling Rajesh Khanna only mimed the songs, and the actual singer was Kishore Kumar – a popular playback singer and actor also from Mumbai. I was still fascinated by the actor. We started collecting scrapbooks of posters and any news or picture we could find of him. We bought Film Mags Stardust, Movie, Picture Post, etc., and still have scrapbooks we made and cherished. Like all of us, my cousin Sushma Sagar who resided at Windsor Road, Ilford, was also a crazy fan, and she had the best collection. So, on visits to their house, we would pinch some photos or a poster. I am sure she knew and found out but was too decent to tell us off or confront us about it. We were just kids but naughty. Our other cousins, Riya and Coogie Kumar were also fans and had their collections. These collections had to be guarded with utmost security. Everyone wanted to get their hands on them.

We, youngsters, were all converted fans by now, and the grown-ups were already following the heartthrob.

Every time a Rajesh Khanna film was being shown at the theatres, we demanded more passes from the organisers as two were, by now, not enough for the growing legion of fans. In 1972, the BBC dedicated a documentary to Rajesh Khanna and his Superstardom called 'Bombay Superstar.' This showed the crazy fan following that Rajesh Khanna had and the hysteria that he created.

In early 1972, our cousins, the Kalia brothers, decided to show Indian films at The ABC in Ilford – now Prabha Banqueting and on the roundabout near the Police Station. They announced that Rajesh Khanna would make a special appearance at the cinema for publicity for his new film, *Dil Daulat Duniya,* showing in the theatre. There were long queues outside the theatre and around the corner. When we arrived, it was clear that the movie would start late and that not everyone would see it. Was a riot expected? The Kalias had made a fortune on ticket sales, and everyone assumed Rajesh Khanna would arrive from Mumbai.

The film finally began late and was well received by the audience, with many claps and whistles and girls going crazy, standing up whenever Khanna appeared on the screen. We will never have another experience quite like this. Nobody compares to Rajesh Khanna. In the early part of that golden decade, Hindi film producers, desperate for 'dates' from Rajesh Khanna, would often remark while referring to him, *'Upar Aaka, Aur neeche Kaka!'* (God is up there, and Kaka is down here.) Rajesh Khanna's nickname was Kaka.

Anyway, they had announced that Kaka would appear during the interval. However, Rajesh Khanna was not present during the intermission. When asked when he would arrive, the promoters said, *"He'll be here soon. He'll be here soon to meet you all."* The audience was buzzing with high-fever anticipation.

Then suddenly, an announcement was made, *"Due to a friend's death in Mumbai, Rajesh Khanna cannot attend the Cinema."* Screams of people echoed in the theatre, girls began to cry, and the audience decided to protest and express their displeasure to the promoters, our cousins, and the Kaila's. People demanded their money back despite having seen most of the film. It took 45 minutes and promises of refunds to calm everyone down. All felt the absence of Rajesh Khanna, and some even believed the excuse made by the organisers.

We knew it was a publicity stunt to bring people to the theatre and make money, but we went along for the ride. We kept following the Superstar and amassed many pictures and stories.

In 1971, Rajesh Khanna visited my Uncle Joginder Sanger's offices in Maddox Street Hindustan Travels, London. Unfortunately, because I was unaware of the visit, I missed out on the opportunity to meet him.

In June 1983, Tony, me, and a group of friends travelled to Mumbai. My brother, Surinder Kumar, aka Tony, from Frankfurt, decided to take a brand-new Mercedes to India.

He asked if I wanted to accompany him to Mumbai, as the car was scheduled to arrive by ship at Mumbai Port. Ajit Prasad, another close friend of ours, also joined us. We flew into Mumbai on Pan Am and stayed in Juhu with another friend, Ali Khan Bhai, directly across from The Sun n Sand Hotel.

It was a fantastic opportunity to meet Rajesh Khanna and other Bollywood celebrities in Mumbai. I tried to contact the actor because I wanted to meet him. We stayed with a friend in Juhu, Ali Khan, who knew a young up-and-coming actress named Rabia Amin, the mother of Jiya Khan, whom it is reported was suspiciously murdered. He introduced me to her, and she was familiar with Rajesh Khanna. When I first met her at Ali Bhai's house in Juhu, I assumed she was just being polite. But, lo and behold, she dialled his number in front of me and made plans for us to visit Ashirwad, a magnificent sea-facing bungalow on Carter Road.

On a sunny and hot Mumbai day in June 1983, the time was set for 11:30 am, and my wish was about to come true. We were driven to his house by Rabia Amin and asked to wait in the front bar area. I was a little nervous, hoping he would be pleasant and meet my expectations, and I did not wish to be disappointed.

Rajesh Khanna was back on the rise in 1983 and reigning supreme. With the super hits 'Souten' and 'Avtaar,' he tasted success once more, as he had in the early days,

Rajesh Khanna, dressed in a pink kurta dhoti, entered the room a few moments later. He appeared to be in good shape. He was having a great time with the release of his new movie, Souten and his phone was ringing with congratulations from everyone. He was cordial and delighted to meet me. We had a casual conversation about his career and upcoming films. I recall being offered tea and snacks. We were there for about an hour and a half.

Then my brother, Tony, arrived with the new Mercedes 230 D that we had brought from Germany. The car pulled up outside Ashirwad's gates, and the horn blared, making a loud noise; Kaka asked, *"Are they with you?"* *"Yes, it is my brother,"* I replied. He requested his people to invite them in as well. Three more people had arrived at the Superstar's meeting.

I recall the first thing Tony said to Rajesh Khanna was, *"You are the greatest actor,"* and he praised him nonstop. Rajesh Khanna enjoyed the praise; Tony had made a good impression of himself. After that, the actor admired the Mercedes and even hinted that he might be interested in purchasing it. I would have given it to him if it had been mine.

I bought my camera and asked if we could take some photos, and he enthusiastically agreed. We said our goodbyes after a few pictures and decided to keep in touch. He liked us, and our reception was friendly and warm. We had high expectations for his style, charm, and softly spoken voice, and he delivered in spades.

"You meet nice people through nice people," he once said, and I'll never forget that. Rabia Amin was a celebrity who kept her promises. She then took us on a tour of Mumbai during our visit.

We planned to stay in Mumbai for a few days after our new car, a Green Mercedes 200D, had cleared customs and all the paperwork had been completed. We had meetings in Delhi and decided to drive overnight from Mumbai to Delhi. Tony, Ajit, and I were all looking forward to this journey as it was thought to be difficult, with steep hills and winding roads.

In June 1983, Mumbai was extremely hot and humid. The heat was harsh, so we left at night when the weather was more relaxed. Ajit took the wheel first while Tony sat in the passenger seat. He was familiar with driving in India and the shenanigans of highway drivers, like the way they turned on and off their dipper lights.

Tony took over driving from Ajit at around 2 am while I was on watch, and we were about 4 hours out of Mumbai on our way to Delhi. Heavy trucks were moving goods on the roads, which were pitch black. At that hour, there were very few cars on the road. These trucks were overflowing with goods, only a few lights were working on their vehicles and very bare street lighting, if any, existed on the journey. They were probably used to driving in the dark, and it was, however, a hazard.

Tony was now driving, and Ajit and I were in the back. Ajit was resting after driving for quite some time, but I was wide awake.

Suddenly, a truck appeared in the middle of the road right in front of us. It was broken down, with its spare wheel jacked up underneath the truck's back end to keep it upright. No lights were working on the truck. Tony, for some reason, did not notice. I, however, did as I was awake and admiring the journey to Delhi. *"Tony, watch out in front of you,"* I yelled. He slammed the brakes, and the car skidded into the back of the truck at around 100 kilometres per hour.

Tony was shocked out of his mind, his seat had moved forward, and the steering wheel was close to his chest by this time. We quickly exited the vehicle and dragged Tony away from the vehicle. I was afraid the car would explode, but I forgot it was a diesel vehicle.

The Mercedes was four feet under the truck; luckily, the wheels positioned under the truck saved the day, as the Mercedes hit the large rubber tyre and bounced slowly back.

Tony was still in a slight shock, and the fact that the car was a total loss hurt him even more. While all this was happening, the truck's occupants slept in the front cabin, unaware of the accident.

It was probably around 4 am, and we needed to devise a strategy. We decided that the damaged car would be loaded onto a truck and transported to Delhi by road. Tony, Ajit, and I took a cab back to Mumbai Airport and a flight to New Delhi to receive the damaged car. It was later repaired.

In early 1983, while working at Empire Travel, Pan Am GSA in Southall, I was approached by Raj Singh, a former Indian cricketer who was now collaborating with Bollywood playback singer Lata Mangeshkar, One of India's all-time successful artists. He was planning a concert tour for the first time in the United Kingdom for Lata Mangeshkar and Kishore Kumar – Bollywood's best male playback singer. Kanti Patel of London promoted the show. We met at our Piccadilly offices, and he insisted that Pan Am be the airline they used for travel.

Since hearing him for the first time in the 1969 film 'Aradhana,' starring Rajesh Khanna, Bollywood's first Superstar, I've considered Kishore Kumar one of my favourite Indian singers. This was an opportunity not to be missed. I went out of my way to secure this agreement and offered lucrative discounts to ensure the ticketing business for the concert troupe. I was able to provide additional inducements of upgrades and excess baggage. It was considerable revenue for Pan Am, and just the endorsement from Kishore Kumar and Lata Mangeshkar would be awesome.

For the first time on stage in the United Kingdom, this would be a concert unlike any other. We covered all the details, including extra baggage and upgrading to Business Class. Kishore and Lata, the two stars, were to travel First Class, complete with all the VIP service.

I arranged with my Pan Am friends to meet both stars at Heathrow Airport on their arrival, and I also hired a photographer to document the arrival. In those days, getting an Air Side Pass to meet an aircraft wasn't tricky. Nowadays, it is unheard of.

First, Kishore Kumar arrived dressed in a brown Kurta, white trousers, shoes, and a warm white hat with his wife, Leena Chandavarkar, and their one-year-old child, Sumeet Kumar, in her lap. Who knew that years later, in 2016, I'd be arranging concerts for Amit and Sumeet Kumar, Kishore Kumar's sons? I presented them with flowers on their arrival, they seemed pleased. Second, there was Lata Mangeshkar and Party, whom I met inside the Pan Am 747 plane and escorted out of arrivals. To mark the occasion, my camera crew was present.

The concerts were sold out, and it was a once in a lifetime opportunity to see Bollywood's best on stage, singing evergreen songs. The performance enthralled the audience and significantly impacted my life, and I have an extensive collection of Records, VDOs, CDs, DVDs, cassettes, and other media. Music is medicine for the soul, bringing out the best in people and making them feel at ease. Musical words can tell stories and have various meanings for people worldwide. The utmost belief is that music can lift spirits, as it lifted mine when I was a child.

As I turn the pages of my mind, Elvis Presley, The King, also significantly influenced my life. I began following his career when my brother Ashok gave me his record 'Let's Be Friends' as a birthday present on February 15, 1969, when I was six, and I have vivid memories of that day.

These were the times of unrest and the Vietnam War; in April 1968, Dr Martin Luther King, a champion for Civil Rights, was gunned down on a hotel balcony in Memphis, Tennessee. Robert Kennedy, aged 42, was running for president of the US and was the younger brother of John F Kennedy, the former president who was assassinated in 1963 in Dallas. In August 1968 was shot and killed at the Ambassador Hotel in Los Angeles. In the US, there was much upheaval and mistrust in the country's state of affairs. Great political leaders snatched away from society, and for what purpose? Why? These leaders, I am sure, had they lived, would have made the world a better place for all.

In 1968 Elvis Presley decided to return to appear before a live audience, even though in 1961, he had done a charity concert to raise funds for the USS Arizona Memorial at Pearl Harbour, Hawaii, Honolulu. Elvis performed at a benefit concert that raised more than $60,000 for the memorial fund on March 25, 1961.

Elvis sang a song that concluded the TV special, dressed in white and singing straight into the camera, 'If I Can Dream', inspired by Dr Martin Luther's legendary speech 'I have a Dream' from August 1963. Elvis was always careful not to sing messages into his songs, but times were different now, and America was headed into uncharted waters. If I can dream, it was a massive hit both in the US and the UK, and the hit record managed to calm tension across the US. After that, Elvis went into the Las Vegas years and continued touring across the US, but only travelled within the shores of America.

My favourite Elvis films are 'Loving You' 1957, 'King Creole' 1958, 'Blue Hawaii' 1961, 'Kid Galahad' 1962, and 'Change of Habit' 1970. My favourite songs of Elvis are 'Don't Be Cruel' 1956, 'It's Now or Never' 1960, 'Can't Help Falling in Love' 1961, 'I Got Lucky' 1962, 'If I Can Dream' 1968 and many more.

Cliff Richard, Bing Crosby, Frank Sinatra, Bobby Darin, Dean Martin, Nat King Cole, The Beatles, Michael Buble and Ed Sheeran are among the singers I admire. Whenever a song is played, the words must have meaning and fulfilment. Its lyrical value is essential to me and should have a lasting impact on the ears that hear it.

Roger Moore, John Wayne, Stewart Granger, Errol Flynn, James Stewart, Clint Eastwood, Muhammad Ali, Jerry Lewis, and Robin Williams are celebrities I have followed and admired in Hollywood.

I loved going to the cinema. Our local cinemas were the ABC in Ilford, The Odeon in Gants Hill, and The Odeon in Forest Gate. Our Green Lane neighbour, Martin Hughes, got us to the movies, and we saw some great films, including Doc Savage, Herbie Rides Again, Michael Caine's The Italian Job, On the Buses, and many others.

I love to watch Roger Moore's The Saint, where he played Simon Templar and The Persuaders, in which he co-starred with Tony Curtis. The streets would be deserted when these shows aired. Furthermore, Lee Majors as The Six Million Dollar Man, The Champions, Thunderbirds, Captain Scarlett, Stingray, and Lost in Space are also my favourites. I also enjoyed watching American television shows like Dallas, Dynasty, Starsky and Hutch, and Happy Days, Henry Winkler as The Fonz and Ron Howard as Richie Cunningham, now one of Hollywood's top directors.

I saw the Bollywood superstar Rajesh Khanna again when he performed with other celebrities at The Royal Albert Hall, but he had hurt his ankle and was in pain. However, he was pleased with his performance during our brief phone conversation. The concert was sold out, and the audience adored his performance. He danced in pain while reciting famous dialogues from his films.

Mr Gurcharan Sagoo of Ranees of Whitechapel organised a meet-up for the stars in Croydon, Surrey, in 1985, and I was invited to attend. Rajesh Khanna and Tina Munim were both present, and I had a good chat with them. Rajesh Khanna recalled my visit to Ashirwad, his home in 1983 with Rabia Amin. I was glad he remembered it.

The meeting was documented with photographs. I had asked my cousin Raj Kumar to meet the Superstar because he was a huge fan.

In 1987, Mona and I decided to take a vacation to Mumbai and invited Bunti, my brother-in-law from Phagwara, to join us.

In Juhu, we stayed at The Sun N Sand Hotel. However, the journey would have been complete with a meeting with the Superstar. So, we made several phone calls but were unable to locate him. Fortunately, I recalled his home phone number, Mumbai 531117, and I found him in Versova after some research. He was staying there while his home, Ashirwad, was being renovated.

After a few days of following my lead, we finally spoke and agreed to meet at his offices on Linking Road in Mumbai. The building was tall, and his private offices were on the fourth floor. I told Mona and Bunti to stay in the car while I exchanged greetings, after which I would call them to meet with Rajesh Khanna. I was ushered into his office, where he was sitting behind a large desk, looking radiant in his trademark white Kurta Pyjama suit. He gave me a warm welcome and a big smile.

We talked about his glory days, and I suggested he start a Rajesh Khanna fan club in the UK and Europe, which I would be happy to run. He still had a sizable fan base all over the world. I stated that my wife and brother-in-law were also present and waiting in the car. He immediately summoned an orderly and instructed them to go and fetch both of them. Mona and Bunti were surprised and had a great time with the superstar, and photographs of the historic meeting were taken.

Rajesh Khanna always struck me as friendly and soft-spoken. Unlike many Bollywood stars who suffer from celebrity hangovers, he was always polite and willing to engage in conversation. He had an affection for his fans and admirers.

Recently, we have connected with Rajesh Khanna's younger sister Kamlesh and her husband Mahendra Makan, they both reside in London, and we have similar interests and enjoy each other's company.

In May 1983, Bollywood superstar Amitabh Bachchan visited London for a series of concerts at Wembley Arena. His manager, Kirit Trevidi of New York, arranged for me to meet him at the Inter-Continental Hotel in Park Lane. We had booked his Pan Am flights for his tour.

SRK – Shah Rukh Khan, we met at The Washington Hotel in Mayfair, and both Megha and Ektaa, my daughters, got to meet him and photos of the meeting were taken. Shah Rukh Khan, I found to be pleasant and friendly and we met again at the Nehru Centre in London, where he was invited to speak.

In 2003, my family and I visited Elvis Presley's Graceland in Memphis, Tennessee, to commemorate my 40th birthday. A dream come true for me. We stayed near Graceland at the Days Inn Hotel on Elvis Presley Boulevard. We visited Elvis's birthplace in Tupelo, Mississippi, Sun Records, where Elvis cut his first record, 'That's all right'. I was keen to meet some of Elvis's inner circle of close friends, mainly from around Memphis. I tracked down Red West, based not so far from Memphis. I got his number from a local Memphis resident. We agreed to meet for tea at the Peabody Hotel in Memphis. Mona, Megha, Ektaa and I were excited, and in walks Red West with his wife, Barbara. They were both very warm and friendly, and we spoke for close to two hours whilst having tea and cookies. We agreed to stay in touch, and he told us stories of Elvis that only one of his best friends would know. It was a memorising time and well enjoyed. Many of my unanswered questions about Elvis and his life that day were answered in full. I was over the moon and well satisfied. On top of that, we met Red and Barbara West, who were just a terrific couple. Red had gone to school with Elvis at Humes High School. Once, some older kids wanted to cut Elvis's hair as he grew them long. In walked Red and said to the kids, if you cut his hair, you'll have to cut mine first. Red was powerfully built, and the kids at school looked up to him. That's how the lifelong friendship between Elvis Presley and Red West started. We came away with some beautiful photos of all of us.

I had the privilege of meeting Jerry Schilling, another close inner circle friend of Elvis in Los Angeles, where he stays in Hollywood Hills in a house that Elvis had gifted him, as he had never had a place of his own. Jerry knew Elvis from 1954 when they played touch ball together in Memphis. He lives with his wife, Cindy an American Airlines Steward. We were attending the wedding of our close friends Naresh and Shobha Dhawan's son, Jitin. I knew Jerry lived in Hollywood Hills, but I had no address. I did some detective work, and through the hotel concierge, I tracked him down and off Mona and I went in a cab. We pulled outside the house, and Mona refused to step out of the cab, saying she did not wish to embarrass herself. She stayed in the cab, and I went to the front door and rang the doorbell. The door opened, and it was a lady. I introduced myself, said I had come from London to meet Jerry and say hello. She said she was his wife Cindy, and that Jerry was out but was in town, He had gone to the studio, working on some Elvis TV movie.

Cindy invited me into the house, and I explained that my wife Mona was in the cab, as she had felt embarrassed to come to the door with me. She laughed and said, please invite her in. We sat down and got comfortable, thinking Jerry could walk in anytime. Cindy was lovely and explained that they both had married in India a few years earlier at the US Ambassadors' residence and that they loved India. They had Indian artefacts displayed in the house. We had some soft drinks, and Cindy took down our hotel number and said she would ask Jerry to call once he returned. I thought how unlikely that was to happen in my mind. But as Mona and I walked into the hotel room, the phone rang, and it was Jerry Schilling. Apologising that he was out when we called by. I explained that we travelled from London for a friend's wedding and that if he were free, we would love to take them both out for dinner. He said he would love that, but Cindy would be travelling. We could meet at an Italian restaurant at the bottom of Hollywood Hills. Another dream was about to come true, and we met that evening for dinner with Elvis's closest friend Jerry Schilling. As we parted company, we had some photos taken as a sweet memory.

We arrived early to be on time and as per time, Jerry walked in, and we made the introductions. Jerry was tall, slim built and smart looking. I recall he wore a blue blazer and blue jeans. We had a full dinner and some red wine and enjoyed his company. He showed us a green, emerald ring that Elvis had gifted him, and he told us some wonderful stories about his friendship with a guy named Elvis. We parted company and agreed to keep in touch. A year or so later, I sent Jerry and Cindy a statue of a Buddha, which they both enjoyed and displayed in their home in Hollywood Hills. Jerry was a true friend of Elvis till the end, there was never any doubt of that. Jerry Schilling wrote a best-selling book on Elvis, Me and a Guy Named Elvis - My Lifelong Friendship with Elvis Presley. Believe me when I state as a fact that this book was not written for financial gain but to set the record straight of all those untruths told by many about the Real Elvis Presley. This was Jerry's way to set the record straight once and for all and to curtail those rumours and myths for those millions of Elvis fans across the globe, who will be forever grateful. The book was a hit and well-received.

The Self-Realization Fellowship at Lake Shrine lies a few blocks from the Pacific Ocean, on Sunset Boulevard in Pacific Palisades, California, in USA. It was founded and dedicated by Paramahansa Yogananda, on 20th August 1950, and is owned by the Self-Realization.

Whilst in Los Angeles we visited the Self Relation Centre in Santa Monica. This is a place where Elvis Presley visited regularly for calm and spiritual meditation. The Lake Shrine Meditation Gardens are open free of charge and Lake Shrine has a contemplative retreat facility where individuals can experience in silence, while enjoying ocean views.

As a fact, The Meditation gardens at Elvis Presley's Graceland in Memphis, Tennessee were inspired by The Self-Realization Fellowship at Lake Shrine and its calm and peaceful persona. Elvis wanted his own meditation centre at home.

Mona, Megha, Ektaa and I visited The Self-Realization Fellowship at Lake Shrine and spent several hours there wandering the gardens immaculately landscaped, the windmill, the gift shop, and the place of worship. It has a surreal feeling of contentment and peace of mind. The gardens are dedicated to all religions and there are different statues of Gods placed around.

In recent years, Megha and Ektaa arranged a surprise for me to meet Priscilla Presley after Elvis in Concert at the O2 Arena. This concert was excellent, with an image of Elvis on a large screen, with members of his original TCB, taking care of business, from the 1970s playing live to his greatest hits. It was so real, and the arena was packed with Elvis fans of all ages. Elvis's appeal to each new generation is unique. All age groups were present.

Suresh & Rajesh Khanna Ashirwad June 1983

Suresh & Rajesh Khanna Ashirwad June 1983

Tina Munim, Suresh & Rajesh Khanna @ London 1984

Suresh & Rajesh Khanna @ Linking Road Office Mumbai 1987

Suresh & Shahrukh Khan @ The Nehru Centre

Shailaja Subramanian, Sumeet Kumar, Amit Kumar & Suresh in London 2016

Suresh, Priscilla Presley & Mona @ Elvis in Concert 02 UK

Ektaa, Suresh, Red & Barbara West, Mona & Megha in Memphis 2013

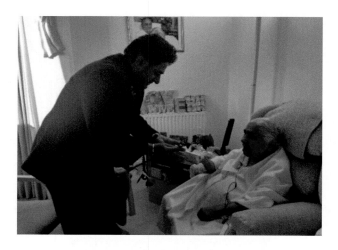

Suresh & Global Head of Brahma Kumari Janki Devi May 2019

Suresh & Babul Supriyo
@ New Delhi 2019

Sourndro & Soumyojit
Kolkata Stars 2018

Joy Bhowmik, Navin Kundra, Suresh & Ketan Kansara 2019

Mona, Arijit Singh & Suresh

Patti Boulaye & Suresh @ Ilford Charity Fund Raiser

Suresh, Zeenat Aman & Mona
@ Charity fund raiser for Nazia Hussain

Suresh, Saif Ali Khan & Mona

Suresh & Tauseef Akhtar   *Dharmendra & Suresh*
@ Indra Travel   *@ Acton West London*

Chapter 9

In God I Trust

Since I have come of age and experienced life's ups and downs, I can say that there is no better decision-maker than God. I have always believed that the Almighty has better plans for us. And I have constantly felt his presence as if God has a particular purpose for me. He has been the one who took care of me through all my good and not-so-good days.

This is not only true for me, nor am I any special or different from others. God is the one who wants to save us from the worst and shows us signs to avoid certain situations. We might feel that we are going through a hard time, but there is a possibility that God saved us from something worse or wants us to learn something that will be useful later in life.

Life is a journey, and it's all about making the right decisions at a given moment. I am not saying that bad decisions or mistakes make us bad people, and I believe our mistakes allow us to improve and learn to stand when we fall. But it is also essential to be wise and quick enough to grab the opportunities God provides us.

At times, when I felt helpless and lost, he guided me and motivated me to succeed and move forward for a better beginning. That's my faith and should be yours too in God, the Man in the Blue Sky.

My parents taught me to be god-fearing, respect one's elders, and treat all people equally. In simple words, we are introduced to having good family values, a foundation and a strong connection with our religion since our childhood. I firmly believe that one God Almighty watches over all of us.

Following these teachings, we were taught to help those in need and help everyone we could. For those less fortunate than us, I have tried my best to do the same throughout my life. While doing such deeds, I feel God has been a guiding light in my life all this time.

Thinking about it, I recall when I was fortunate enough to marry Mona. All the odds were stacked against me, but it was what I wanted, and circumstances were created to make it happen. It was not me, but God guided and supported me, and I had the will and conviction to make it happen.

It's not that I have never gone through any bad times just because I have done good deeds. Even my faith, like others, has been tested several times thus far in my life, especially when I lost my mother to cancer in 1981 and my father to liver cancer in 1993.

Auntie Prakash passed away in 1995 due to cancer, and my Uncle Varinder, a happy-go-lucky man, enjoyed all that life had to offer. He enjoyed the company of his brothers and family and gelled well with the younger generations. He was a well-loved member of the family. He suddenly and sadly passed away in 1998 due to a rare illness.

Another death in the family which affected all of us was of our cousin, who died young. Our cousin Keshav Kalia, once of Sam Travel and subsequently left and set up an independent business and worked closely with Aeroflot. A full-of-life talented young man passed away at the age of 39 whilst exercising in the gym. He had a severe heart attack. He loved to dance like John Travolta and admired Bruce Lee. A tragic loss for his family and all who knew him.

Once again, I faced the death of Punam Kumar, my sister-in-law and Tony's wife, who died on 6th August 2000 of a brain haemorrhage. Tony, Punam, Mona and I were at our friend

Rajinder Johal's party at Westrow Gardens, Seven Kings when she collapsed on the dance floor and died. It just goes to confirm how unpredictable life can be. She had many plans and wanted to see her children settled and married. This was a significant blow to the family. Leaving three young girls behind, Tina, Reena, and Esha, who have since grown to be incredible women, successful and hard-working in their own right.

Subsequently, in 2005, Tony remarried Gulshan Ahuja, an advocate from Chandigarh, Punjab. Loving and devoted, she has done a fantastic job and settled well into the family. She would have done well if she had continued her lawyer career path. It's never too late, she may start again in time.

The death of loved ones, coming to terms and moving forward always hurts. In 1987, my brother Ashok married Renu from New Delhi at the Ashoka Hotel, with grand wedding celebrations. They settled in Frankfurt, Germany and raised a son Akash, a motivated young man with high-spirited, hard-working and entrepreneurial skills. Sadly, in later years, we lost Ashok due to a sudden and unexpected death. The death of a brother is never going to be easy and leaves a void in all our lives.

There were times when I began questioning the existence of God and his meaning, and I felt like I was losing my faith in him during some exceptional times in my life. Injustice in everyday life is widespread, and in every circle, one has to face it now and then, but fighting for our rights is equally important. Never accept any injustice.

Chapter 10

Amit Kumar

Music is a universal language and some people become successful at a given point in time. And as time passes, vogues, fashion and styles change, these people either die or wither away and new people step in. The only ones that we remember are those who were not just successful, but who did something unprecedented and took their art to another level. Their contribution changed their field of craft for coming generations.

S. D Burman was a father like figure to Kishore Kumar and supported his career and Amit Kumar idolised R D Burman, aka Pancham. Both the Burmans were musical genesis of Bollywood Hindi Cinema. S. D Burmans music was more traditional and classical, whereas his son's music was contemporary, largely western in form and featured instruments not widely used in India and always thinking out of the box. R D Burman introduced a new sound, with a new sensibility and new beats. Their music remains fresh today, as ever. R D Burman could create sounds out of everyday things that we use in our daily lives. He was a maverick and a musical genius.

R D Burman suffered a heart attack in 1988 and underwent heart bypass surgery a year later at The Princess Grace Hospital in London. He left for London without a word to anyone, as he did not want anyone to be concerned or worry. When his close friend Rajesh Khanna found out, he was livid, that R D had not informed him of the operation. He took the next Air India flight for London from Mumbai and went immediately to the hospital.

R D was surprised and pleased to see his friend Rajesh Khanna. He was a true and loyal friend till the end. In 1994, his life was cut short, and he died of a severe heart attack, at the age of 54.

I followed Bollywood from the young age of six. Meeting Rajesh Khanna and Kishore Kumar was already an honour for me. Then I met Amit Kumar, a well-known celebrity who was a playback singer and entertainer in Bollywood. He was the son of legendary Bollywood playback singer Kishore Kumar.

I first met Amit Kumar at a concert at Watersmeet in Rickmansworth. This concert was held in September 2012 in the UK and was arranged by Pankaj Sodha.

Earlier in August 2012, I'd had an accident and fell, so my ankle was broken, and I had to use crutches to move around.

As soon as I learned about the concert, I decided to go. I did not want to miss the chance to see Amit at any cost. I bought two tickets and asked my brother Krishan to accompany me for support as I was still recovering from the fall. I was strongly advised not to travel to the concert, as the journey may cause more damage to my already broken ankle. But, being determined, I was not going to miss the Amit Kumar concert. It was worth the trouble.

We arrived nice and early at the venue, and Bankim Desai had arranged some aisle seats for us up front. It was a packed hall, and I was excited. This was my first-time seeing Amit Kumar live in a concert with his brother Sumeet, the son of famous Bollywood actress Leena Chandavarkar, the lady who became Kishore Kumar's fourth wife.

I know this might be somewhat confusing, but those fans of Kishore Da realise he was married four times. His first wife was Ruma, a Bengali singer and actress, and she was the woman who gave him his first child, Amit Kumar. Then he got married to Madhubala, of Mughal-e-Azam fame. After that, he married Yogeeta Bali, and finally, his last marriage was to actress Leena Chandavarkar who gave birth to his second son, Sumeet Kumar.

You might wonder why I called him Kishore Da and not Kishore Kumar. "Da" is a Bengali word used to show respect after a name, and because Kishore Kumar is a credit to Bollywood, people usually refer to him as Kishore Da to show respect.

At the concert, Amit sang some of Kishore Da's evergreen classics. His voice was unique, and I found it quite like that of his father. Then he sang some of his hits, along with Sumeet, who sang some of the old Kishore classics. As the intermission approached, I was excited to meet Amit Kumar and introduce myself to him.

I managed to get on the stage and into the side wings, where the changing rooms were situated. I was with Krishan, my younger brother, who ensured I did not fall off the stage. I managed to push myself up with the crutches. I knocked and entered the room, introducing myself to the son of the music legend.

Amit met us with a warm smile, and we started to chat. I told him I had met his father in 1983 in London and that we had made all the travel arrangements for their tour. When he had come to perform at Wembley with Lata Mangeshkar, he was delighted to hear that. We talked for about 15 minutes before it was time for him to start his show.

I was surprised to see how laid back he was and that he had come prepared for the shows. After meeting him, I decided I wanted to do a show with him in the UK, and I could sense that he wasn't too pleased with the promoter's arrangements. We agreed to stay in touch, and Prakash Dictokar, his manager, and I exchanged numbers and kept in touch.

A dear friend of mine, the King of Bollywood shows in the UK, Vijay Bhola of Rock on Music, was keen to be involved in a show with Amit Kumar, and Vijay had been arranging top-class Bollywood shows since the 1970s. We decided to team up and do two UK concerts, one in London and the other in Leicester, where both Kishore and Amit Kumar had large fan followings.

The London show was to be held at Logan Hall, Holborn, on 22nd October 2016, and the Leicester show at De Montfort Hall on 23rd October 2016. The show was called 'Yeh Shaam Mastani', a reference to the famous song Kishore Da sang in a film starring Rajesh Khanna, named Kati Patang. On 19th October, we held an audience with Amit Kumar at the Nehru Centre, and it was a question-and-answer session, which was well-received by the audience.

Mrs Vibha Kapoor, Deputy Director of the Nehru Centre, was very helpful during this event. On 20th October, Amit Kumar was to be the first Asian to receive an award from the Houses of Parliament for his 50 years of service to the Indian film and music industry. This was to be presented by Keith Vaz, Member of Parliament for Leicester.

We were given a VIP tour of the House of Parliament and Lords, which was appreciated. Mr Virender Sharma MP, Ealing Southall, welcomed us and joined us for the tour. Amit often talks fondly of those memories, and the award is displayed front and centre in his awards cabinet at Gauri Kunj, Kishore Kumar's home in Juhu, Mumbai.

The concerts were sold out and were a hit. Amit Kumar had a growing fan base in the UK and had been performing there since 1972 when he came with his father for the first time. I was a bit surprised when Amit told me that his passport looked like a club sandwich which had grown over the years due to his travels around the world to concerts and tours, referring to his Indian passport.

We raised Amit Kumar's profile, and the newer audiences were getting to know and hear about him. The earlier UK concerts and chat shows had received good coverage, thanks to Teji and Natasha of Sterling Media, TV coverage by Neeraj Arora and Miyrah Mistry from Sony TV, radio coverage by Tony Lit of Sunrise Radio and Tari and Sujatha Sian of Nu Sound Radio, and Amba of Sabras Radio in Leicester. Our sponsors were Sanjay Anand of Madhu's, Samson Sohail from Cobra Beer, Kailash Singh of Air India, and others. Ashvin Bhai of Videorama in Kenton was one of our main ticket agents. Many more supporters and friends contributed to making these shows a runaway success.

Once we had held the first set of concerts, Amit Kumar and I developed a good understanding and trust. Thanks to Prakash, the manager, things became more accessible, and they knew I always had Amit Kumar's best interests in mind. I wanted him to be a more giant star than he was and more commercial in his outreach to audiences.

We began to brainstorm and saw how this might be possible. We had to make a bang and think out of the box, doing something that no one had done before, something unique that no other Bollywood artist had done. I aimed to showcase the voice that sounded close to his father Kishore Kumar.

So, I decided to plan a few concerts in different parts of the UK. I wanted to support local artists from within the UK as well. Because I believe the UK has lots of unseen home-grown talent.

I brought Ketan and Anji Kansara on board, a husband-and-wife team who worked well together. Ketan was a Bollywood singer inspired by Kishore and Amit Kumar, and Anji was a talented woman who did design and artwork. I had gotten to know Joy Bhowmik of Eastern Euphony, another Bollywood singer who idolised Kishore and sang his songs. Now, these people would support Amit in concert, but I had to convince Amit. I explained that I wanted to support local UK artists to encourage more to come forward. This would be a great platform to achieve this. Amit wholeheartedly agreed and thought it was a good idea.

We were going to start at the Becks Theatre in Hayes, Middlesex, on 14th June 2019, and then move on to The Queens Theatre in Romford, Essex, on 16th June. From there, on 17th June, we went to the Nehru Centre.

Amit Kumar was pleased with the informal and close setting. The audience was cheering and enjoying Amit's presence and singing. Many of them were going crazy, excited to be so close to Amit Kumar in concert.

Another presentation was held at the House of Parliament with Bob Blackman MP, Lord Navnit Dholakia, Keith Vaz MP, and Councillor Anjana Patel, who had assisted in setting up this event. The room was packed to the rafters, and it was a significant interaction with the invited audience. After that, Amit Kumar received an award for his continued service to the entertainment and music industry.

This award was presented by Bob Blackman. After this, Prime Minister Theresa May had to make the presentation but was called away at the last moment, so Bob stepped in to do the honours.

We had a corporate event, Amit Kumar, in concert at the Heston Hyde Hotel in Heston on 21st June, partnering with Sanjay Anand MBE of Madhu's. It was a runaway success, and the corporate audience had a great time.

On 22nd June, at the Heston Hyde Hotel, Bhupesh Raseen, Rajesh Khanna's right-hand man, had flown from Mumbai to the UK to participate in the informal segment before the concert. He wanted to share his experience of being with Bollywood's first superstar Rajesh Khanna.

Initially, I chaired a Question and Answered session with Bhupesh, which led to Amit joining us on stage and telling some untold stories and singing. It would make this concert exciting and different from others. The audience loved this segment, and Bhupesh recollected the golden moments in the superstar's life. It was jam-packed.

The last date of the UK Legacy Tour 2019 was at De Montfort Hall Leicester on 24th June. We had decided to send the band and others ahead in a bus while Joy, Amit, Prakash, and I drove up separately.

Amit loved to have McDonald's now and then. This was one of those days, and I wasn't surprised at all, being aware of his likes. We drove to McDonald's and got takeaway.

As we reached Leicester, we realised we were early. We decided to take advantage of the extra hours. Amit got ready and began rehearsals with the band. Soon, we were all set to go.

Amit is a humble person. He loves his fans and is always ready to meet them, so before the show, we set up a meet and greet backstage in the dressing room, which the fans enjoyed. On this occasion, famous UK singer Navin Kundra, and his wife and parents, had come to the show and came backstage to get some photos taken with Amit.

The audience consisted majorly of Asians who loved the show and shouted out plenty of song requests during the performance, and Amit was pleased to oblige. We had a lively audience that night in Leicester, and the fans were singing along. It was 11:20 pm when we wrapped everything up and drove back to London.

Amit doesn't like hanging around with people after his concerts. He usually feels exhausted and wants to return home as soon as possible.

Well into the journey, I got a call from Vijay Bhola of Rock on Music in the early morning. He told me that a terminally ill cancer patient who was a fan of Amit Kumar was requesting a birthday wish from him. He couldn't make it to the concert because of his illness. By now, some of us in the car were already asleep.

I was in the front passenger seat and noticed that Amit had awoken. I told him we needed to do some heavenly work and record a special message for a cancer patient. Without a thought, he said we would do it on arrival at Heston Hyde Hotel. The car pulled up in front of the hotel reception at around 2:30 am.

I could sense Amit was exhausted from the tour. He told me we should record the message since we were still outside the hotel. We recorded his message on my phone and sent it to Vijay.

I pray it made a slight difference to the patient, and Amit's small, gracious gestures made him more enduring.

The next day, 24th June, we woke up fresh. After a good night's sleep, it was time to pack and prepare for the journey back to Mumbai. Amit was feeling ill and exhausted from his hectic tour schedule.

We can't ignore that he is in his late sixties, into his autumn years, despite looking much younger. We called a doctor to examine him, and he was fine, but he needed rest to regain his energy levels.

Air India Regional Managers, Kailash Singh, Tara Naidu, Debashis Golder and Anil Maken; Air India, LHR, as usual, was fantastic, and all the meet-and-greet arrangements were flawless, with boarding cards already in hand. A big thank you to my friends at Air India, Surekha, Vimal, Suresh Solanki, Shashi, Cyrus, and Manjiri. Some Air India personnel have committed and dedicated lifelong services to the company.

Amit Kumar was returning to Mumbai to see his wife Reema and family, who were missing Amit. Indeed, he has a family who loves him a lot.

The UK Legacy Tour 2019 was a runaway success. The results were beyond my imagination. It felt like we had accomplished the impossible. It was like a dream come true. I could not direct his father, Kishore, in concert, but I more than made up for it with Amit and Sumeet. The hard work of every person paid off. The audience loved the concerts, and we tried to make each show different by changing songs. One of the highlights was a special segment called Tribute to the Legends, Amit Kumar's special tribute to the legendary singers of Bollywood, consisting of tributes to Mohammed Rafi, Mukesh, Manna Dey, K.L. Saigal, Hemant Kumar, and most of all, his father, Kishore Kumar.

The audience was surprised that Amit was such a versatile singer. Many of them couldn't believe it when he sang the songs of such great artists just like them. This was a practice he was to keep in future shows worldwide.

My first visit to Kishore Da's Gauri Kunj house was in 2019. Mona and I were visiting, and we were going to meet Amit Kumar and discuss preparations for the UK Legacy Tour with him. We were both given the VIP tour by none other than our dearest friend Amit. He showed us around, and we discovered all the different rooms in their house. He even told us stories about his father. As we walked into the front garden, he showed us where his car Ford model A, which was used in the hit film Chalti Ka Naam Gaadi, had been buried by his father, Kishore Kumar.

Soon we were introduced to Ruma Guha Thakurta, his mother, who was in her bedroom watching cricket. She was in good health then, and Amit introduced us to her, and we talked for a while.

Our visit went well. The day was filled with laughter and joy, but after a few months, the unexpected news of the death of Ms Ruma was aired on television. Who knew the woman we had just met would leave this world so soon?

When we heard the news of the passing of his mother on 3rd June 2019, in Ballygunge, Kolkata, we were all shocked and wanted to call Amit. I rang Prakash, his manager, to see how he was taking this sad news and to see if we had to push back the start of the tour.

Prakash had spoken to Amit, and he had said, "The show goes on. The one who had to pass on has moved on."

These days were difficult for Amit. He was very close and fond of his mother, and they had spent much time together. She was the first woman in Kishore Kumar's life. Amit had a great time with his parents and was quite attached to them. After his father's death, his mother was his only solace, but her passing shattered Amit.

Yet, he was professional and knew he had to go on, even though the death of his mother had shaken him to the very core. He was deeply grieved but didn't show it to anyone. The man had millions of fans, yet I can't imagine how lonely he might have felt after losing his mother.

After a while, I spoke with Amit, gave him our condolences, and wished him to stay strong. I reassured him that this unfortunate time would pass. He asked about the shows and the ticket sales, and I confirmed that all was well and that ticket sales were going well.

Amit taught me never to let such things affect our lives. If the situation is out of our hands, we shouldn't complain or cry. Instead, we should accept reality and move on. This is how it works.

In conclusion, over the years, I have always tried to inject some local UK talent into our concerts and offer them an opportunity to take centre stage. I have had the privilege to work with some of the top UK artists, Micky Sethi, Joy Bhowmik, Ketan Kansara, Sanjoy Dey, Chirag Rao, Ani Bardhan, Urmi Chakraborty, Anu Shukla, Indrani Dutta, Rikta Mukherjee, Bali Brahmbhatt, Manisha Sharma, Anil Khadi, Nidhi Shrivastava and UK's most successful Navin Kundra; we still await to collaborate. We arranged themed concerts, such as Yeh Shaam Mastani, Crazy for Kishore, and Zindagi Ka Safar, all focused on the legendary Kishore Kumar and Rajesh Khanna.

Amit & Suresh @ The Madhu's Sheraton Skyline Hotel 2017

Suresh, Amit Kumar & Loveena Tandon of Aaj Tak TV in London 2016

Kishore Kumar, Amit Kumar & Suresh
Gauri Kunj Mumbai 2019

Suresh & Kailash Singh
RM Air India

Suresh, Ektaa, Amit Kumar, Mona & Megha @ Queens Theatre 2019

Bob Blackman MP, Presenting Amit Kumar 50 years' service to Indian Music Industry & Suresh @ House of Commons 2019

Suresh, Bhupesh Raseen, Amit Kumar, Channi Singh of Alaap, Bob Blackman MP, Mona, Cllr Anjana Patel and friends celebrating Amit Kumar 50 years' service to Indian Music Industry @ House of Commons 2019

Chapter 11

R C A/The Kumar Foundation

In 2000, the Conservative Mayor of Redbridge, John Lovell and his wife, Janet, approached me to assist in the New Year's Day Parade entry. In a short time, I got several people involved in Honey Kalaria from Honeys Dance Academy, the Business Community for some financial support and others. The New Year's Parade is a highlight, and London's 32 Boroughs tend to participate. They would have a theme for the float, which would be decorated, and have colourful displays, vehicles and dancers befitting the theme. The Redbridge theme was Redbridge through the Ages. We had a Winston Churchill look-alike in a Rolls Royce waving to the crowds. Honeys Dance Academy dancers were in colourful costumes displaying multi-culturalism and Bollywood. We had some Irish Dancers and Bhangra Dancers. A music deck with several prominent speakers was fitted onto the long lorry to give a unique sound effect. Time slots are allocated to each entry, and they join the procession at a given entry point and time into the parade. We got the Redbridge Drama Centre involved with students and musicians participating and seated on the lorry. We had a brass band and much enthusiasm. A panel of judges mark each entry on size, theme, colour, and appearance. At around 5 pm, the results were in.

Redbridge had won first prize, a large trophy displayed in the cabinet on the first floor at the Ilford Town Hall and a cheque for five thousand pounds towards the chosen charity of the Mayor of Redbridge. Everyone was delighted, and John and Janet were very grateful for my support and presented our team and me with Certificates of Merit. Those hang proudly in my offices at Indra Travel.

Over the years, I have supported many Mayors of Redbridge, regardless of political affiliation. I am a member of the community of Redbridge first, and that's all that matters.

The New Year's Parade route is usually along Piccadilly, Westminster, and Hyde Park. Over one million spectators watch it along the roadside along the way of the parade and telecast to millions across the world.

My parents have instilled a profound value in coming forward and helping the needy. It was vital for me to participate in raising awareness and assisting charities actively. During my political campaigning, I came across many local charities doing excellent work.

I set up Redbridge Cultural Association and Redbridge Community Awards (RCA) to support local charities. Some charities we have helped over the years include:

- Haven House Hospice – Woodford

- Focus Club for the Blind

- Leukaemia Cancer Research

- The Orchid Cancer Appeal

- King George Hospital – Baby Rainbow Appeal

- Melting Pot

- M S Society – Chadwell Heath

- Polio Children

- The Ilford Hospice Chapel

- PDSA Animals Charity

- The Chinese Association of Barking

- Various Redbridge Mayors Charities

These funds were raised from various events, such as the Redbridge Community Awards or donations from the business community. We also raised funds from auctions and raffle tickets at various events. These events were supported by high-profile guests, such as Lord Jeffrey Archer, Patti Boulaye, High Commissioners, politicians, businessmen and others.

Many community groups who supported and volunteered their services by performing include the Irish Dancers, the Israeli Dancers, Honeys Dance Academy, and other singers and dancers.

The Kumar Foundation was established to support worthwhile causes. It was inspired by the Aamir Khan Bollywood movie Taare Zameen Par, based on a young child with dyslexia. We wanted to highlight the unique needs of children and speak about the problem of lack of education in India and other countries. There is much poverty around the world, especially among children, impacting their access to education. We aimed to support those causes.

We arranged a Kumar Foundation Charity Football Tournament at Elmbridge Club, Hainault, in Essex. Football was central to my life, and I had much confidence from playing the game from 5 to 16 years old. It had given me pleasure and enjoyment. I loved everything about the game, it is fun when one tries to snatch the ball from their opponent and score a goal. Honestly, I miss those days. But this was my chance to get football back in my life. And so, I did!

We arranged a five-a-side knockout competition with sixteen teams from the local community. The age groups varied, but it was more for enjoyment and fundraising rather than stiff competition. The winners were the Mann Family from Seven Kings. They played to honour their grandfather, Darshan Singh Mann, a lifelong community worker in Redbridge and East London. Mr Mann was a father-like figure who was one of the early founding members of Barking Gurdwara in Barking, Essex and the Punjabi Centre on Ley Street, Ilford.

We raised around three thousand pounds for the Redbridge Mayors Charity. I was surprised to see how much we were able to collect. I saw the good in charity and how it can assist people. Even those people contributed from whom I was expecting the least. Gradually, I could feel inner peace and happiness in giving and doing good work.

The world we live in today has been through much change, from world wars to pandemics, but one thing which has remained constant throughout is resilience and kindness. Kindness towards nature, animals and other people can transform the world and make it a beautiful place to live. Still, it is important to remember that compassion towards you is essential for personal growth.

Moreover, it is the spirit to fight back and help each other. Kindness is an essential and universal quality to improve the world. I recall the famous Michael Jackson song 'We are the World.'

Honey, Mayor John Lovell, Suresh, Mayoress Janet Lovell & supporters

Supporting The Mayor of Redbridge Maureen Hoskins

Suresh with Lynda Clarke at Haven House

Some recipients of Our Charity Fund Raising at Redbridge Mayors Parlour

Supporting the Boy Scouts of Havering

Supporting The Muslim Disabled Association with Abida Iqbal

Friends of The Ilford Hospice Chapel

Funds raised for The Chinese Youth Association

Supporting Melting Pot Charity and Members with Salim, Khalid & Paul Waraich

The Apna Elderly Group of Ilford Mr Sudharsan Bharjee, Sansar Singh Narwal &
Members

Suresh, Mona & Colin Osbourne MBE of The Orchid Cancer Appeal

Chapter 12

The Gate of Peace

For thousands of years, people have erected monuments. Monuments are objects or structures built to commemorate a significant person or historical event. In many cases, they are symbols of ancient civilisations, like the pyramids in Egypt or the Parthenon in Greece. These monuments were so massive that they required the labour of thousands of people.

Monuments have become well-known city landmarks over the last two centuries. The Statue of Liberty in New York welcomed European immigrants to the New World, and the Eiffel Tower in Paris was built to mark the entrance of the World Fair in 1889.

However, there is a difference between monuments and memorials, and people often need clarification on the two. Memorials are built to honour the death of a known figure or loved one, such as soldiers killed in a battle or an important historical figure, like the Lincoln Memorial in Washington, D.C. Similarly, Mount Rushmore in South Dakota is one of the most well-known memorials. It is a sculpture of famous presidents' faces carved into a mountain.

The World Trade Centre Memorial at Ground Zero is one of the most recent structures, commemorating thousands of people killed in the 9/11 terrorist attacks. Memorials do not necessarily have to honour just those who were dead. They can also be erected in memory of loved ones who passed away.

In India, it is common to have monuments and memorials built in memory of passed loved ones. This is very common in Punjab and northern India, and the Taj Mahal is one of the best and most famous examples.

From what I've seen and know about northern India, it is regular to see such statues and gates built in loving memory of those who have passed. When you drive through the streets and villages in Punjab, you can see various gates, mainly at critical points, like an entrance.

My dad, who was born and raised in our village, always longed to visit Kitna and did so whenever he got a chance. He was kind and loving toward his fellow villagers and was one of the first people in line when it came to helping others. He hated it when people were discriminated against based on caste, colour, culture, wealth, social status, or other characteristics. Those who knew him were aware of this side of his. He strictly followed his religion and culture.

My father wished to have a gate named in memory of his parents, Shri Kali Sharan, and Smt Banti Devi, in his village in India called Kitna, located in the Hoshiarpur district of Punjab. Like me, he had seen monuments constructed to memorialise loved ones or a special event in the village, and he wanted to do the same for his parents.

He loved his parents and appreciated all they had done for him. I remember my father telling us that it was almost impossible to repay all his parents had done for him. Now that I think about it, he was right. And his statement isn't valid just for his parents but for all those who struggle and toil just so their children can have a better life.

After the death of our mother, Indra Bhardwaj, in September 1981, our father was deeply grieved. His one and only companion, whom he had promised to stay with forever, was gone. In the Hindu culture, there is a concept of reincarnation, according to which a person is reborn.

After mom's death, our father took a step back from day-to-day work. He gradually lost interest in everything and wanted to spend more time in the village and Delhi. Maybe he wanted to relive moments of his childhood and youth.

As a result, he visited Kitna more often and spent most of his time with his friends from the village. He tried to help and assisted those in need with financial support, etc,. Thinking about it, he realised that there was still something left for him to do. He remembered his desire to have a gate erected and positioned at the entrance of the village Kitna. He had been planning it for a long time now.

"Kitna in Hoshiarpur is some forty-five minutes away from Phagwara city by road, two hours from Amritsar, one hour from Jalandhar, and one and a half hours from Ludhiana," he told us whenever he talked about our village.

The family house in the village Kitna belonged to our grandfather Kali Sharan. At the premises, above the door, there is a plaque in Urdu with my grandfathers name written Kali Sharan, and after his death in 1965, it was handed down to our father and his two brothers, my uncle Varinder and uncle Naresh. My father would never sell the house and wished to retain it or put it to use for the community and people of Kitna.

This one is the most memorable among many acts of generosity and kindness in my father's lifetime. A lady named Kausalya lived in the village of Kitna and had three young children. Her husband had died, and she had nowhere to go. Being a widow with three little kids, she was scared and had no idea how she and her kids would survive. She was hesitant and couldn't trust anyone.

When my father learned about her from the local people of Kitna, mercy filled his heart, and he gave her permission to stay in our family home with her young children. It was an act of kindness and charity. I remember my father telling us she didn't agree to stay at first, but when she met him, he convinced her by telling her it was better to stay there than to wander the streets with three children.

Our father was a humble man who always kept track of his origins and roots. He always remembered those days of poverty when he had little money and struggled to make ends meet. Dad agreed with the lady. She could stay in the house with her family, and in return, she could take care of the house and greet our guests whenever someone came. She had to open the door for them, ensure the house was clean and tidy, and offer refreshments to those who came to visit. He did this so the woman wouldn't feel burdened.

To this day, this lady continues to keep up her end of the agreement. Currently, her children's children live in our house with their families.

Each time anyone from the family visits, they are always met with a smile and warmth. The visitors, often from the UK, offer small donations or gifts to the family.

For the visitors of our family, it is an opportunity to show their children or grandchildren where their original roots were. Many people visit the village and our house, and that's the only real mark of remembrance left.

We also had another land near the house, but that has been lost over time. There were some mango tree orchards in Kitna, but I'm not sure what happened to those. The sad thing is that when dad fell sick, he kept thinking about the gate he wanted to erect but couldn't, and his sickness took away all his strength.

Therefore, in 2003, I was committed to fulfilling my father's wish and constructing the gate. I decided to name it the Gate of Peace. I had asked my two brothers-in-law, Bunti and Ashoo Sharma, to look after the project and take care of the building with workers from Phagwara. It was ready, as per my specifications and design plans. The work took around four months to complete.

Bunti and Ashoo did a great job overseeing its development. The inauguration stone was laid by the Deputy Superintendent of Police in Jalandhar, Navjot Singh Mahal, a loyal and dedicated police officer.

The Gate of Peace is dedicated to Shri Kali Sharan, Smt Banti Devi, our Grandparents and Pt Kul Bhushen, and Smt Indra Sharma, our parents, committed by all six brothers and inaugurated by myself, Mona, Megha, and Ektaa.

The Gate of Peace is a solid structure finished in green marble with a red slated roof. The foundation is made so travellers can rest on its plinths. Each year, it needs to be renovated and cleaned. During elections, local people use the gate as advertising columns.

When it was completed, we returned and held an event and a *Puja* for the people of Kitna. Each year a Janmashtami *Puja* is held at the temple in August for the people of Kitna in memory of our grandparents and parents. A special thanks to Praveen, a resident of Kitna, for his support and service to the people.

It was a priority for me to keep our links to Kitna. Our parents wished to remain in touch with the village, so I will go for as long as I live. I am glad we managed to carry out my father's wish, and the Gate of Peace was built for the people of Kitna to see and for us to remember and mark the existence of our ancestors.

The Gate of Peace in Kitna Punjab in memory of grandparents & parents

The Gate of Peace in Kitna Punjab in memory of grandparents & parents

Chapter 13

Family & Friends

Always Forever

A friend is one that you can count on at any time. In a lifetime, one has a limited number of real friends. You will meet people and have business associates along the way. But they are not your real friends.

Friends, you can count on the fingers of one's hand. Knowing they will answer your call, you can pick up a phone and call these friends day or night. They are rare, and you find them along your life journey.

You can laugh with them, share a joke, and open up with your inner thoughts. Look for advice and guidance, knowing that they will only have your best interests in hand.

They stand with you, during your highs and lows, without being judgemental. You can choose your friends, but not your family.

A supportive and loving family is a blessing. The nurturing and care your family raise you with, becomes the foundation for your life journey.

I am very grateful indeed and consider myself fortunate that I have a great family and friends, whose support has helped me through thick and thin.

Indra Travel was established after the passing of my mother, Indra, in 1981. I wanted her name to be forever eternal in the community. We have seen success and will forever remain grateful to our clients and friends who have supported us. It is because of them all that we are who we are today. Over the years, we have always maintained reliable customer service and offered competitive prices. Our personnel at the office will always make that little extra effort to please and make the customer comfortable. Many of our clients we have gotten to know as friends. I have seen grandparents, parents and children who have grown up in front of our eyes. The younger generation, at times, will recall the days they accompanied their parents to our Travel Agents at Romford Road, Manor Park, to book flights and holidays. A special thanks to Satish Parmar, Shefali Mehta and Tony Newman at Indra Travel who have given many years of service and loyalty and remain in place. I also wish to acknowledge my sincere gratitude to all the personnel who have worked with us over the years.

Raj, my elder brother, and Urmil have two daughters. In 2005 Kavita and Rahul Pushkarna successfully went into Bollywood film production with a super hit film, Page 3, which won three National Film Awards, including the Golden Lotus Award for Best Film, directed by Madhur Bhandarkar. The storyline is based on a journalist working for a tabloid who frequently visits high society parties and discovers the superficial and dual lives of celebrities and the hypocrisy and insecurities they live with. Ritu and Mark Sapsford, after working with her father Raj, in travel and aviation, ventured into stocks and shares successfully.

My brother Raj's younger son and my nephew Bob Kumar commenced his career in travel and tourism and subsequently ventured into hospitality and established Little Bay and Tapas Bar in Ocean Village, Gibraltar, on the border of Spain. Bob married Raju in 2009, and she found the Gibraltar restaurant and pushed Bob to make the deal. It turned out well for them. It is the finest Indian restaurant with many Accolades and Awards bestowed. It is frequently visited by locals, tourists, visiting celebrities, royalty and politicians. His success has come from loyalty, determination, commitment and hard work.

Krishan, my younger brother and I are very close, and he has always stood by my side and has supported me in all that I do. We have enjoyed many good times together. Whilst growing up we shared a mutual love for football and sports. We have both grown up listening to the music of Elvis Presley and watching his movies. Krishan is married to Sharmila, and they have three wonderful children, Shivani, Akshay, and Amman. Shivani is in education and teaching; Akshay is an actor and has starred in various films and TV series, such as Homeland, The Indian Detective, Legends, and The Halcyon, to name a few, and Amman is very active in sports and has ventured into the world of business and commerce. All worked hard to succeed, I am proud of them.

My father, mother and my father's brother and wife were both two brothers married to two sisters. Riya, Coogie and Raj were my first cousins, and we were close, whilst growing up and remain close even today. Raj aka Gog my first cousin is an entrepreneur and he and I used to travel to Empire Travel in Southall, in the 1980s when he was learning the ropes of the Travel and Aviation business. We spent good times together. Raj is compassionate and has done much within his family to secure younger members into business and to establish themselves. Married to Fiona and blessed with two daughters Taniya and Natasha.

Coogie, my first cousin and I have always been close, and I recall she would visit so that I could teach her some Mathematics, I tried my best, but she did not realise that it was not one of my finer subjects. My report cards were really nothing to write home about. She is an IT consultant and is well travelled. She is married to Pierre and has one son Luka.

Riya, my first cousin, always reached for the sky and had big dreams of success. She has a strong mind and is determined to reach the top of her game. She works in Travel and Aviation and has worked hard and established a successful business. She is married to Rahul and has two children, Ria and Rohan.

As youngsters, growing up in Seven Kings in the 1970s, one of our regular to do, was to watch horror movies on a Friday night on ITV. The Hammer House of Horror. The regulars were Dracula, starring Christopher Lee and Peter Cushing, The Werewolf, with Boris Karloff, The Mummy and Frankenstein. We would wrap ourselves up in blankets and make howling noises to scare each other and at that age, they were frightening to watch. Those were the days, and those memories are clear today, as they were yesterday.

As I look back over the years, their parents Uncle Varinder and Auntie Prakash would be proud of them and their success.

Uncle Naresh and Auntie Swarna had two daughters Suman and Roman. Raksha Bandhan in Hindi means "the bond of protection". A universal Indian festival celebrating the relationship between brothers, cousins, and sisters. It involves the tying of a Rakhi (the sacred thread) by a sister on her brother. There is a ritual of tying the Raki on a brother's wrist. They would both tie Rahki on me and my brothers each year and we would give a small money gift. One year early in the morning, it must have been around 8 am, whilst I was rushing to get to a meeting in London, the doorbell rang and I was in the bathroom shaving. I ran downstairs to open the door, and it was Suman and Roman. Rather than greeting them to come in, foolishly I suggested they tie a Rakhi on Surinder aka Tony first as at the time he lived at 12 Norfolk Road, just down the road from us at 69. And return after that and tie it on Krishan and me. They looked at me and walked away. They in fact had taken offence, that I had shooed them away unknowingly. This was the start of many years where they refused to visit and tie a Rakhi on me. But they continued to tie the Rakhi on my brothers.

After several years and whilst watching a popular Hindi Bollywood movie from 1971 titled Hare Rama Hare Krishna, starring Dev Anand, Mumtaz and the glamorous Zeenat Aman, a popular song called Phoolon Ka Taaro Ka was sung by the evergreen Kishore Kumar. The composer is Rahul Dev Burman and the lyricist is Anand Bakshi. The song was filmed about a brother and sisters love for each other. Phoolan Ka Taroon Ka, which translates to Flowers and Stars always forever. It just hit me that this was wrong and that I should do something about putting this relationship back to normal. I jumped into my car, at the time a Mercedes, and went to my brother's office in Cranbrook Road, to discuss the issue and there I saw Roman tying a Rakhi to Raj, my elder brother. She was surprised to see me, to say the least. I said well it's my turn now and she obliged, as she was put on the spot. I gifted her. Then off to Suman's home. I rang the doorbell and there was no answer, although I did see some curtains move. I dropped a note in the letterbox and left, that she should call me urgently. After a short while she did, and I returned and had the Rakhi put on my wrist and gifted her. I was glad that the relationship was back to normal and to this day it continues with respect.

Since childhood, Ajmer Singh Mann aka Manni and the Mann family have always been supportive. They are family friends. Most of the family live in Seven Kings, and from my football days through to politics, Ajmer had stood firm. I will be forever grateful.

Paul Waraich, originally from Amritsar and a Chartered Accountant, businessman, and renowned community worker, has been a constant support over the years.

Khalid Hussain, the owner of K1 Tyres in Ilford Lane, is another friend who can be called upon to stand tall. He has done wonders with the South Ilford Business Association, 'SIBA,' and transformed Ilford Lane during the past 30 years.

In 1989, our Pan Am Sales office was situated at 35 South Road, Southall and Madhu's were based two doors away at number 39. Madhu's was run by my friend Sanjay Anand MBE, his father Madhu, and other family members. They had newly opened and wanted support to promote the restaurant. I was happy to oblige and shifted all my dining and parties to Madhu's, from the Maharajah restaurant, which was based on Broadway in Southall.

Madhu Anand was a jolly fellow, well-experienced in life and a bigger-than-life character with a flare of a Bollywood Star. Madhu loved jewellery and wore plenty of gold rings and necklaces. All our Pan Am parties were held at Madhu's and any entertaining. His passing was a sad loss to the community, and over the years, Sanjay has developed Madhu's into an international brand with the help of his family. From early beginnings in Southall, Madhus under the stewardship of Sanjay, has grown to 5 UK locations. Arjun, Sanjays son has been a breath of fresh air for the business and during COVID, when many businesses were facing ruin, Madhus embarked upon an aggressive expansion mode. That's called taking a challenge head on and the policy has proven to be successful. It was a great honour when Sanjay was awarded the MBE by Her Majesty Queen Elizabeth II for services to hospitality.

Balbir Singh Walia, businessman and a friend for 40 years, since the days of my first car, Ford Escort 1.6 Ghia. One fine morning my Ford Escort was hit by a careless motorist on South Road, Southall, and I took it for repairs to the Walia Motors garage at The Green in Southall. This started a lifelong friendship of trust and mutual respect. I recall our regular chats and openness about life and the future.

I met Keith Prince, politician, during his by-election to Barkingside Ward, and we instantly became good friends. I have watched his career progress over the years. First, being elected as A Councillor, then becoming a cabinet member, I was part of the team that helped him become leader of Redbridge Council, and now he is a London Assembly Member. Whilst others turned out to be fair-weather friends during difficult times, Keith was one of the few who stood by my family and me. Keith has been a good and loyal friend.

Another solid friend over the years has been Carl Lindley of the Metropolitan Police Service. Whilst I was a Councillor for Valentines Ward in Redbridge, I met him at Area seven committee meetings. At one such meeting, where the public was becoming unreasonable towards the police, I stood up and defended his comments, which were fair and reasonable. At times the public expects too much from the Police. While in Redbridge, he did some sterling work with neighbourhood policing to improve trust locally and work across businesses, faith groups and ethnic differences. My sincere gratitude for the friendship.

Friendship, to me, is the family members in life that you get to choose. They are the ones that stand by you in tough times and help you celebrate the good. Loyalty, support, understanding and trust are all words that are synonymous with friendship. In summary:

"There are big ships and tall ships.
And they all sail the sea.
But the best kind of ship is friendships.
And they're the ships for me!"

"A friend makes it easy to believe in yourself." "A good friend is like a four-leaf clover; hard to find and lucky to have." "The language of friendship is not words but meanings." "Find a group of people who challenge and inspire you; spend much time with them, and it will change your life."

A close friend is honest and speaks from the heart with good intentions. They tell you what you need to hear in a way you can listen to rather than gossip behind your back. A quality friend is trustworthy; not only are your secrets safe with them, but so are your vulnerability, fear, and weirdness.

You create a strong bond with close friends who want the same thing in life – to live a happy life and be surrounded by happy people. Real friends share laughs, memories and inside jokes. They share your good time and increase the feeling of happiness when you achieve anything significant in life.

Friendship means a bond between people that connects them and lets them share each other's feelings and thoughts. Someone is your friend if you feel like you can tell them anything and you love to spend time with them.

Healthy relationships play a pivotal role in general happiness. People are healthier, happier and less stressed when they have good friends to lean onto.

These bonds are essential because family helps us get through the most disastrous and best times. Family is important because they can offer support and security coupled with unconditional love; they will always look to see and bring out the best in you, even if you cannot see it for yourself.

My family has always meant a great deal to me from an early age when I was growing up. It stemmed from the love I received from my parents and brothers, which has grown with me and continues to get intense with time.

Family is essential in one's life and the foundation of one's being. But there must be a clear understanding between all members, as too often misunderstandings do occur, and relationships become strained. Sometimes much time is spent on small quarrels and misconceptions rather than clearing the air and clearing up matters. It is said that one can select their friends, not their family. So, you are stuck with your relatives. That's why building more vital bridges among the family is essential. Strong families express appreciation and affection. Strong families have a solid commitment to each other. Strong families spend enjoyable time together. Strong families manage stress and crisis effectively. Strong families have a sense of spiritual well-being.

Our families teach us how to live our lives the right way. They teach us how to solve our problems with honesty and love, show us how to see the best in any situation, and exemplify what it means to love somebody with all their heart. Several characteristics are generally identified with a well-functioning family. Some include support, love, and caring for other family members, providing security and a sense of belonging, open communication, making each person feel important, valued, respected and esteemed.

Joginder Sanger the son of Jamna Das and Lakshmi Devi of Apra, Punjab. He married Sunita and had two children, Reema and Girish. My mother Indra's younger brother and my uncle.

He is the Chairman of the Mastercraft Group of companies and is considered one of the UK's top Hoteliers. The Hotel collection includes the Washington Mayfair Hotel, The Bentley, Courthouse and Heston Hyde hotel. In 1997, their first purchase was the Washington hotel in Mayfair after he consolidated his property portfolio; the purchase was instigated by his daughter Reema. By now, she had completed the Hotel and Management course. As the first hotel, it was a heavy investment, he was nervous and restless as the business flourished slowly. Seeing her father restless, Reema asked him to stand outside the Washington hotel, wrap his arms around it, and give a big hug. That broke the anxiety at home.

Since arriving from Apra in 1961, he worked various jobs to make ends meet. In 1967 ventured into travel and aviation.

He supported the Indian Workers Association and the Hindu Society in South London. He was Chairman of the Indian Sports and Cultural Association to promote Kabaddi and Punjabi hockey and a leading light of Balaji Temple near Birmingham, which supports the Indian Vedic culture and traditions as well as inter-faith harmony. Singh Sabha Gurudwara in Southall, the Hindu Forum of the UK and Indian Gymkhana Club in Hounslow and others have benefitted from his generosity and support. He is an authentic Indian and believes in traditional family values and hard work.

He was one of the early pioneers to commence Air India Charters to India and established BOAC. In 1973 he was appointed Air India GSA in the UK, and he termed the phase

GSA – General Sales Agents, which means sole rights to sell airline tickets on behalf of the airline. Air India's Regional Director was Maneck Dalal, who was also the Chairman of The Bhavan and suggested in 2011 that uncle be appointed Chairman of The Bharatiya Vidya Bhavan. He was elected, with his contacts and new style of work, managed to raise much-needed funds to secure the future of the Bhavan.

It was time to hand the baton to his two children, Reema and Girish. With both comfortable in the saddle, he went on to leisurely pursuits. Uncle is always available to give guidance. He now enjoys his Autumn years and spends time with his wife, Sunita and their grandchildren.

There is a saying that behind every successful man is a woman. This statement cannot be more accurate where Sunita Sanger is concerned. She has stood alongside her husband and was instrumental in many of the hotel's internal designs and decorations. A pillar of strength for her family.

He has received several Awards and Accolades in his lifetime for his generous philanthropy and community work. He is known to family and friends as Panditji, which in English means wise man.

Family means having someone to love you unconditionally despite you and your shortcomings. Family is loving and supporting one another even when it's not easy. It's the best person you could be, and you may inspire your loved ones.

I am fortunate to have a good circle of friends consisting of successful businesspeople and entrepreneurs, and I believe this is the true wealth one accumulates in one's lifetime. The key to maintaining relationships is to be available to those who matter, help where you can, and not take anyone for granted.

Sanjay- MBE, Chairman Madhu's and Reena Anand. Dalip, formerly with HSBC – Head of Multi-Cultural Banking and Sonia Puri. Tony- MBE, of Sunrise Radio, the UK's number one Asian radio station and Mandy Lit. Samson, Head of Global

Sales - Cobra Beer and Usha Sohail. Neeraj Head of Sony TV UK and Neha Arora. Daljit, formerly with Jaguar UK and Surbjit Jagait. Sandeep of Frontier Raas – Southall and Simi Sarna. Sanjiv and Ritu Gandotra, originally from Chandigarh and now living in London. Mansukh Property Developer and Geeta Jivraj. Respected Kul Bhushan and Sujata Joshi of Seven Kings.

Rajan and Shalini Sawhney, Consultant and Aviation Expert, formerly with Interglobe Global and Southall Travel. And many others.

Joginder Sanger & Suresh at
Courthouse Hotel London 2018

Suresh, Joginder Sanger & Mona
at The Bhavan event 2019

Mona, Mohoni Auntie - Jalandhar & Suresh

Joginder & Sunita Sanger

The Sharma"s – Phagwara Family

Tony Lit MD Sunrise Radio, Mona & Suresh

Suresh, Mona, Megha, Ektaa with The Makans

Suresh, Megha & Krishan 2014

Suresh and first cousin Anita Kumar 2019

Virender Sharma MP, Suresh, Joy & Mithi Bhowmik

Friends Forever @ Neeraj Daughters Wedding 2020

Suresh & Kul Bhushan Joshi @ Ilford

Friends Forever Keith Prince, Carl Lindley & Suresh

Dr Honey Kalaria and Suresh @ Heston Hyde Hotel 2019

Sanjay Anand & Suresh

Reena, Mona, Suresh & Sonia @ Cricket

The Elite Group Friends

Mona, Ektaa, Prem Kalra & Suresh @ Delhi

Jitin Prasada BJP MP & Suresh

Anirban, Suresh, Mukesh @ Mumbai

Bob, Suresh & Krishan – The Singing Trio

Suresh, PM John Major & Bobby Walia

Suresh, Teji & Ramesh Arora of The Montcalm Hotel

Avinash Kalia, Nipan Bhardwaj & Suresh

Rajesh Kumar Cousin & Suresh

Suresh & Gowri Shankar @ New Delhi

RM Air India Debashis Golder & Suresh

Suresh, Raj, Krishan & Tony at Frankfurt

Chapter 14

Way Forward

I have covered many historical events and circumstances up to 2010. The next phase of my life only confirms how one's life is a twist and turning rollercoaster and how life can change overnight without considering what to expect in one's life.

These circumstances I will cover as a follow-up in my next book.

Thank you for reading my book and allowing me to share my life experiences, from which lessons have been learnt and followed. I hope that, in some small way, you will be able to take something away and avoid the mistakes I encountered on my voyage.

Follow that dream; life is beautiful. Live each day to the full and enjoy it with your family, friends and loved ones.

Adios - Until we meet again in my next book ....

Appendix

Let me explain first, the two families of my parents Pandit Kul Bhushen Jasuja and Smt Indra Bimla Bhardwaj.

Father's parents: Pandit Kali Sharan & Smt Banti Devi

My father's family: 4 brothers and 4 sisters

Brothers in age order:
- Pandit Kul Bhushan Jasuja Bhardwaj
- Naresh, Jagdish & Varinder Kumar Bhardwaj

Sisters in age order:
- Shankuntla, Bimla, Kanta, & Shanta Devi Bhardwaj

Mother's parents: Pandit Jamna Das & Lakshmi Devi

My mother's family: 4 brothers and 4 sisters

Brothers in age order
- Desraj Sanger, Roop Lal, Janak & Joginder Sanger

Sisters in age order:
- Indra Bimla, Prakash Rani, Savitri & Mohani Sanger

Appendix

My father Kul Bhushen Jasuja and Indra Bimla Sharma Bhardwaj's family consisted of:

Six sons - Raj, Surinder, Satish, Ashok, Suresh and Krishan.

His brother Naresh Chander and Swaran Devi Bhardwaj's family, consisted of:
- Suman, Roman, Rakesh, Harish and Mohan.

His brother Varinder Kumar and Prakash Rani Bhardwaj's family consisted of:
- Riya, Ash, Coogi and Raj.

His sister Bimla and Bagwant Kalia's family:
- Om Parkash, Tarsem, Gyan, Manna, Paramjit, Surinder, Gopal and Keshav and Sunita Kalia.

My father's sister Shanta and Vidya Sagar's family:
- Satish, Ashok, Sushma, Rajesh, Rakesh and Suresh Sagar